Instant Style
for Writers

Instant Style
for Writers

Compiled by
Hayden Mead, Ph.D.

Developed by The Philip Lief Group, Inc.

BERKLEY BOOKS, NEW YORK

INSTANT STYLE FOR WRITERS

A Berkley Book / published by arrangement with
The Philip Lief Group, Inc.

PRINTING HISTORY
Berkley edition / January 1997

All rights reserved.
Copyright © 1997 by The Philip Lief Group, Inc.
Developed by The Philip Lief Group, Inc.
This book may not be reproduced in whole or in part,
by mimeograph or any other means, without permission.
For information address: The Berkley Publishing Group,
200 Madison Avenue, New York, New York 10016.

The Putnam Berkley World Wide Web site address is
http://www.berkley.com/berkley

ISBN: 0-425-15546-3

BERKLEY®
Berkley Books are published by The Berkley Publishing Group,
200 Madison Avenue, New York, New York 10016.
BERKLEY and the "B" design
are trademarks belonging to Berkley Publishing Corporation.

PRINTED IN THE UNITED STATES OF AMERICA

10 9 8 7 6 5 4 3 2 1

CONTENTS

INTRODUCTION

The *Concise Guides* series consists of six authoritative reference workbooks for people who need to communicate effectively both in person and on paper, and who need to find reliable answers quickly and efficiently. As many writers have found, most technical manuals are laden with jargon and are poorly organized. However, the basic guidelines and helpful suggestions persented in *Instant Style for Writers* will provide writers of all levels with clear, comprehensive information about writing—in a revolutionary new way. Whether for home, business, or educational use, *Instant Style for Writers* is the handiest style manual available. The first section, "Elements of Style," contains entries on the most important writing concepts, including: different types of writing (*business letters, dialogue*); frequently misunderstood grammatical issues (*semicolon, squinting modifier*); specific word problems (*amount* vs. *number, than* vs. *then*); and acceptable racial, ethnic, religious, and gender terminology. The second section, "Style Quick-Finder A to Z," allows you to find immediate listings to correct spellings (*hors d'oeuvre, Mississippi*), abbreviations (*FYI, NATO*), and fine word choice distinctions (*fiancé, fiancée*). The alphabetical format of both parts means you can find answers to a wide range of questions with ease and speed.

Writing style incorporates a broad scope of things: effective word choices, grammatically correct sentences, logical organization, cohesive arguments, clearly written prose, and well-presented ideas and examples. Style affects the way you present your material and also the way it is understood by your reader. Although most people learn the basics of grammar, punctuation, and organization in school, not everybody learns the more specific elements of style. Writing on a regular basis and reading all kinds of writing—novels, newspapers, reports, brochures, and so on—contribute to your ability to recognize good style. However, nothing can replace knowing the most crucial stylistic guidelines. Whether you are writing a term paper, a chemistry lab report, a business letter, or a work of fiction, you need a guide that will tell you how to put together the most appropriate and convincing words for your purpose. Knowing the basic elements of style, including how to address your reader in the proper tone, will directly relate to your ability to write interesting, intelligible prose. Use *Instant Style for Writers* as a supplement to a good dictionary, thesaurus, and style manual. Polishing your skills will enable you to better communicate with others in business correspondence, school assignments, and oral presentations.

For both home and business communication, *Instant Style for Writers* is the most accessible style handbook on the market. It lists entries alphabetically and provides clear, concise explanations along with useful examples that will answer all of your writing questions. In addition, an extensive cross-referencing system will enable you to find the explanations you need so you don't waste time when you don't know where to look. Everything from *expository writing* to *lay vs. lie* to *circumlocution* is explained in concise, uncomplicated terms in this guide, to help you make your language as polished as possible.

ELEMENTS
of
STYLE

A

Abbreviations
Abbreviations are short forms of words and phrases. If an abbreviation represents one word, omit periods between letters *(Mr., Gov.)*. If an abbreviation represents more than one word, periods may or may not be necessary *(U.S.A., CIA)*. Consult a dictionary to be certain your abbreviations are correct. *See also* **Style Quick-Finder.**

Abstract diction
The heavy use of complex, imprecise words. This type of writing is usually unclear and wordy. If you need to explain abstract ideas, you should use language rich in description so your readers understand the point. Here is an example of abstract diction: *A major theme connecting the findings of the sociologically significant project is a progressive trend toward socioeconomic alienation among the affluent suburban geriatric members of the study's test group.* Here is the same idea expressed without abstract diction: *Research has shown that many elderly people feel alienated by their suburban surroundings.* Abstract diction should be avoided when clear, precise diction can be substituted. *See also* CLARITY.

Active voice
See VOICE: ACTIVE, PASSIVE.

Adjective
Adjectives are words that describe nouns or pronouns. Adjectives are the spice of writing; use them to clarify, describe,

modify, enhance, or specify your nouns and pronouns. Here are some examples of adjectives: _big brown_ cow; _great balls of fire_; _stubborn_ donkey; _two_ visitors; _most_ people.

Adjective phrases function the same way as single-word adjectives, but they are made up of more complex ideas expressed through combinations of words: _The pediatrician, who had had extensive training in the diagnosis and treatment of leukemia, was awarded an honorary title for his groundbreaking work._

Nouns can also function as adjectives: _fern bed_. This is a simple way of demonstrating a more complex relationship: _the bed filled with ferns_. Be careful not to string too many nouns as adjectives in your writing, as this can create confusion as to what is the subject and what is being modified: _Sample computer desktop programs are available._

Adverb

Adverbs are words that describe verbs, adjectives, clauses, or other adverbs. Like adjectives, adverbs intensify and enliven writing by modifying other parts of sentences. They can show degree, manner, place, and time. Here are some examples of adverbs: _he writes_ effectively; sweetly _singing_; she feels well; _I am_ almost _there; she_ then _walked away._

When using adverbs, bear in mind the rule of the split infinitive: Do not place an adverb between _to_ and the verb following it. WRONG: _To barely move._ RIGHT: _To move barely._ While it is best to follow this rule in most cases, if the phrase sounds strange or awkward to you, abandon the rule for fluidity's sake.

Adverbs also indicate comparative degrees of quality. Almost all adverbs form the comparative and superlative by adding _more_ or _most_ before the adverb: _more completely; most completely._

African American

See RACIAL, ETHNIC, AND RELIGIOUS TERMS.

Agreement

There are two main types of agreement that writers need to be continuously aware of: subject/verb and pronoun/antecedent. Always check to be certain that your subjects and verbs agree. For example: *the child eats; the children eat*. Be especially careful when there are phrases or clauses separating subjects and verbs: *the children seated in one large group eat quietly*. Do not be tempted by the singular noun *group* to change the verb *eat* to *eats*; the verb should agree with *children*, which is the subject of the sentence, not *group,* which is just part of a prepositional phrase modifying the subject. Pronouns and antecedents (words that pronouns refer to) must also agree in person and number. Indefinite pronouns such as *either, neither, each, every, no one,* and *everyone* are tricky because they are singular pronouns, even though they seem be plural. The following examples are all correct: *Anybody can bring <u>her</u> dog; Anybody can bring <u>his</u> dog; Anybody can bring <u>her or his</u> dog*.

ain't

Slang word commonly used to express *am not*, *is not*, or *are not*. This is a nonstandard usage that should be avoided in formal writing and speech. *See also* SLANG.

all ready

See ALREADY VS. ALL READY.

all right vs. alright

Alright is not accepted in formal usage. *All right* is an adverb phrase that means "satisfactory. "

already vs. all ready

Already is an adverb that means "by this time": *She is already prepared for the test. All ready* expresses the state of being ready: *She is all ready to go to the mall; They were all ready for takeoff.*

alright

See ALL RIGHT VS. ALRIGHT.

Ambiguity

Avoid ambiguous language. It confuses your readers and clouds your ideas. If necessary, shorten your sentences to lessen punctuation difficulties, or use a thesaurus to locate a more suitable word. Be sure that prepositional phrases, adjectives, adverbs, and other modifiers clearly relate to the proper part of your sentence. This is an ambiguous sentence: *The police officer gave a speeding ticket to the driver that ruined his driving record.* Was the driver responsible for a poor driving record, or was the ticket to blame? An unambiguous revision of the sentence might read: *The police officer gave a speeding ticket to the driver, who already had a bad driving record.* *See also,* CLARITY; CONFUSED WORDS; AND DICTION.

among vs. between

These prepositions are commonly confused because they both refer to more than one item. *Among* refers to three or more things: *among the citizens; among family members. Between* refers to two things: *between* you and me; between the married couple.

amount vs. number

Use *amount* if you cannot count the items to which you are referring, or to indicate an abstract or indefinite size: *the amount of dirt; the amount of rain.* Use *number* if you can count the items to which you are referring: *the number of orders; a number of strange occurrences.*

Ampersand

This symbol (&) stands for the word *and.* It occurs in formal writing only in the names of some companies *(Porto, Zibello & DeCapua, Inc.)* and, in source citations, to separate authors' names. For example:

Corcoran, Richard L., Morris, Richard Y., & Litchfield, Eric J. (eds), *Alternative Rock and the Essence of "Cool."* New York: Lexington Press, 1996.

Note that the comma separating the final ampersand and name occurs only for citations with multiple names, but not in company names with two or more elements: *Simpson & Company*.

Analogy

A comparison used to illustrate an unfamiliar or abstract idea. Analogies link together elements that may be otherwise unrelated as the writer attempts to draw parallels that signify a likeness between ideas or things. For example, if you want to argue the self-sufficiency of the human body, you may make the analogy that the body is a microcosm of the entire earth. When you create an analogy, be sure that your comparison is consistent and appropriate. Don't say that a dog's tail is analogous to a drop of rain unless you are certain that you can make the analogy work.

and/or

Avoid using this awkward and informal phrase whenever possible. If you mean *both*, use *and*; if you mean *either*, use *or*. For example: *The store may be open on Saturdays and/or Sundays* can be more clearly written as *The store may be open on either Saturday or Sunday, or both*.

Anecdote

A short narrative that is usually interesting and amusing. Anecdotes are useful in informal writing and speech as a way to personalize or enliven your narratives. Use them in speeches and introductory passages of some types of writing to break the ice between you and your audience or reader. You might begin an oral presentation on thermodynamics with something like: *"As I sat down to organize my notes for this presentation, I realized that most people have no idea what a thermonuclear reactor looks like, and so I decided to bring along this pamphlet that I picked up at a reactor site in Washington. Let me first tell you about what happened during my tour of the site. . . . "*

Anger

A tone in writing that expresses infuriation or annoyance with the audience. Even if you are writing a letter of complaint, avoid angry tones in formal correspondence. You can accomplish much more by keeping an even temper and expressing your opinions lucidly. There is no reason to write *I absolutely cannot believe that your organization is crooked enough to not refund my deposit* when you could write *I would appreciate a full refund of my deposit before August 31, 1996.* You can work around your anger in business correspondence when necessary; however, anger in expository writing is not acceptable under any circumstances. *See also* BUSINESS LETTER; OPINION.

anybody vs. any body

Anybody is a singular indefinite pronoun, like *anyone* or *somebody.* The phrase *any body* refers to a physical entity; *any* is an adjective modifying the noun *body.* Some examples: *Anybody can sing the blues; Any body not identified will be cremated.* Note that indefinite pronouns take singular verbs and pronouns; *Anybody may speak her mind.* See also INDEFINITE PRONOUN.

anymore vs. any more

Both constructions of the adverb are acceptable in standard English, but *anymore* is more common and perhaps preferable. Example: *It is not raining anymore.* When you are referring to an amount, use *any more*: *Is there any more spaghetti?*

anyone vs. any one

Anyone is an indefinite pronoun that is singular in number and should therefore agree with singular verbs and pronouns:

Anyone might shout out his or her opinion. The phrase *any one* refers to a specific person, thing, or group; *any* is an adjective modifying the noun *one.* Example: *Any one of the many buffalo could charge the rancher. See also* INDEFINITE PRONOUN.

Apostrophe

A symbol (') that shows possession or takes the place of missing letters. An apostrophe and an *s* (*'s*) added to singular and most plural nouns forms the possessive: *Harry's shoe*; *the belt's buckle*; *children's voices.* An apostrophe without the *s* can be added to plural words that end in *s* to form possessives: *workers' benefits*; *three weeks' pay.* When used to show contractions, apostrophes are essentially taking the place of omitted letters. For example, *can't* is the shortened form of *cannot.* The apostrophe takes the place of the letters *no.* In *don't*, the apostrophe replaces the *o*; in *should've*, the apostrophe takes the place of *ha.* Apostrophes can also be used to form the plurals of numbers: *1990's*; *the double 2's. See also* CONTRACTION; *ITS* VS. *IT'S.*

Appositive

A word or phrase that identifies or explains the phrase it refers to: *Joe, my son-in-law, is coming over for dinner.* In this case, *my son-in-law* is an appositive. (You can also say that the phrase *my son-in-law* is *in apposition to* the subject *Joe.*) Appositives are set off from the rest of the sentence by commas, unless the relationship is clear enough that commas are not necessary: *Frosty the Snowman.* Note the subtle difference in these two sentences: *My daughter, Joanne, is five years old; My daughter Joanne is five years old.* The commas enclosing the appositive phrase in the first example indicate that there is more than one daughter and that one of them (Joanne) is five years old; the absence of commas in the second example indicates that there is only one daughter.

Argument

The point that you are attempting to illustrate in a piece of writing that is meant to persuade or convince readers. When presenting an argument, you should begin by clearly stating your point. Then, with logic, reasoning, and examples, support your argument with plenty of evidence to strengthen your ideas and convince readers that your case is valid. *See also* OPINION.

Article

The words *a, an*, and *the* are articles. *A* and *an* are indefinite articles, which means that the nouns they precede are not already understood by the reader. If you write *an apple on a tree in an orchard*, you are not assuming that your reader knows which apple, tree, or orchard. Presumably, you will identify your nouns in detail soon after mentioning them with indefinite articles (*a* and *an*). *The* is the definite article; whenever you use *the*, your reader should already be acquainted with the noun that follows. If you write *the apple on the tree in the orchard*, your reader can be certain that the apple, tree, and orchard to which you are referring are the only ones you will be discussing.

as

This word is not recommended as a substitute for *because, since*, or *while*. Consider this sentence: *As the car slowed down, we decided to stop for a while*. Did we decide to stop *because* the car slowed down or *after* the car slowed down? In usages like this, *as* is often inadequate, vague, or ambiguous. Choose a more descriptive word.

as vs. *like*

Both are used to show relationships or to make comparisons, but *as* is a conjunction and *like* is a preposition. *As* links verbs and verb phrases; *like* links nouns. This is the differentiating factor for the two words. *As* means "serving the purpose of": *She acts as if she were scared*. The phrase *such as* (*I brought food such as pretzels, chips, and dip*) is similar to the preposition *like*. Like, meaning "similar to," is used to form similes: *That man looks like a clown. See also* SIMILE.

Asian
See ORIENTAL; RACIAL, ETHNIC, AND RELIGIOUS TERMS.

Attribution
See BIBLIOGRAPHY; QUOTATION.

Audience
The intended readers of your writing. It is crucial that you know your audience and understand what style, tone, content, and level of writing your readers will expect. Be familiar with their needs and expectations. If you are writing an article for your town's only newspaper, your audience is fellow citizens whose interest in the community's well-being is important to them, their families, and their neighbors; therefore, the style should reflect the interests of these readers. If you are writing a lab report on your biology experiment, your audience is your professor and perhaps other biology students; you should keep the tone formal, authoritative, and accurate. A general audience is comprised of diverse backgrounds; you must use your writer's judgment to determine an appropriate style and tone for a general readership. Ask yourself questions like these: Will my readers expect information, opinion, or entertainment? How much do my readers already know? How much do they want to learn from me? How old are they? What political stance do they take? Are they skeptical or gullible? Are they grading my work? How can I avoid offending them? What is their lingo? What is their humor? What type of a person do I want them to perceive me as? After assessing your audience's expectations and gathering your thoughts, you are ready to begin writing.

Awkward sentence
A sentence that sounds overly formal, confusing, or un-clear. Grammatically, there may be nothing incorrect with an

awkward sentence; however, to the reader's eye, awkward sentences look unusually perplexing and clumsy. Whether it is too long, too short, poorly organized, or unbalanced, an awkward sentence can almost always be rewritten into clearer and more precise prose. These sentences are unacceptably awkward: *You should try to avoid taking the long route to the baseball field, the one going through the center of town and on long blocks. You should walk the easier and shortest way which, I believe, is going through the schoolyard and passing by the gas station.* These could be revised as follows: *Don't take the long route to the baseball field. Instead of taking long blocks through the center of town, simply walk through the schoolyard and past the gas station.*

B

B.C., B.C.E.

Both refer to the same era: the former stands for *before Christ*; the latter stands for *before the Common Era*. Both are acceptable for referring to the period of history before the year 0. Some may want to avoid B.C. for political correctness. The same applies for A.D. *(Anno Domini—year of the Lord)* and C.E. *(Common Era)*. Again, these both refer to the same period of history—the years since the year 0.

because of vs. *due to*

Because of is a prepositional phrase. It is acceptable for explaining reasons or circumstances. Two examples: *Because of his lisp, Johnny was misunderstood; I am late because of my car troubles.* *Due to* is acceptable after a form of the verb *to be*: *The cold weather is due to high winds.* However, when used as a preposition resembling *because of (due to the wind, the weather is cold)*, *due to* is awkward and colloquial. Avoid using it when you mean *because of*. Remember, one may begin a sentence with *because*, as long as the sentence is complete. *Because I am happy* is an incomplete sentence, but *Because I am happy, I smile* is acceptable.

behalf

Both *in behalf of* and *on behalf of* are acceptable usages for this word. Although there is no dictionary-definition difference, there are two stylistic distinctions. Use *in behalf of* when you mean "for the benefit of": *Charles accepts the award in behalf of the Class of 1962.* Use *on behalf of* when you mean supporting or defending: *The lawyer argues on Matt's behalf.*

being as, being that

Both are nonstandard expressions. Substitute *because* or *since* whenever you are tempted to use either of these phrases. There is no need to write *Being that we are usually hungry before noon, let's eat early today* when you can write *Since we are usually hungry before noon, let's eat early today.*

beside vs. besides

Beside is a preposition that means "at the side of": *The table is beside the bed. Besides* is another preposition that means "except" *All of the girls besides Jane want to go to the birthday party.* Although perfectly proper, *besides* has an informal sound to it; be careful when using it in formal writing.

better vs. best

Comparative and superlative forms of the adjective *good.* *See also* COMPARATIVE; SUPERLATIVE.

better vs. had better

Better is the comparative form of the adjective *good. Had better*, as in *ought to*, is a helping verb plus an adverb. The helping verb is necessary and should not be omitted. Never write *It better rain*; the acceptable version of this sentence is *It had better rain*.

between

A preposition expressing the relationship involving two items: *The food is lodged between her teeth.* *See also* AMONG VS. BETWEEN.

between you and I/myself

This phrase is grammatically incorrect. Never use the subjective case *(I, you, he, she, it, we, you, they)* in a prepositional phrase. *Myself* is a reflexive pronoun that can only be used in the subjective case. Prepositions require the objective-case pronouns: *me, you, him, her, it, us, you,* and *them.* The correct phrase is *between you and me.* See also HYPERURBANISM.

Biased language

See RACIAL, ETHNIC, AND RELIGIOUS TERMS.

Bibliography

The list of sources that you cite in your writing. The purpose of a bibliography is to give credit to other writers whose ideas, facts, illustrations, summaries, or words you have borrowed. This is necessary, and legally required, whether you are writing a paper, an article for a magazine, or a newspaper article. Ideas and quotations that are not documented or cited are considered plagiarized. Although styles vary according to the type of publication for which you are writing, the general information cited in a bibliography includes the name of the author or editor, the title of the work, the publishing company or name of the publication, and the year and place of publication. The following set of examples is a guideline to writing a bibliography.

Basic book listing:

Schmo, Joe. *The Mundane Life of a Normal Guy.* New York: The New York City Press, 1996.

Basic magazine, journal, or newspaper listing:
Valley, Lilly. "The Merits of Pretty Flowers." *Hometown News-paper,* issue XXV (1991): pp. 21–22.

Book with two or three authors:
Schmo, Joe, and Ziegfeld, Arthur. *Follies and Fallacies.* New York: The New York City Press, 1996.

Book with an editor:
Dickens, Charles. *David Copperfield.* Ed. Donald Thomas. New York: Penguin Books, 1989.

See also CITATION; FOOTNOTE; PLAGIARISM; AND QUOTATION.

Black
See BLACK ENGLISH; RACIAL, ETHNIC, AND RELIGIOUS TERMS.

Black English
Many schools now recognize Black English as a dialect of American English with its own distinct rules of grammar and style. Some grammatical differences are: subject/verb agreement *(she go, I be);* omitted helping verbs *(he going);* and an absence of possessive nouns and pronouns *(they sweater).* Although Black English has become more widely recognized as a dialect and not a deviation in the classroom, it is still not preferred in places of business. Employers are less likely to respond favorably to cover letters and applications written in Black English than ones written in standard English. For employment opportunities and written communication, it is recommended that business professionals be familiar with standard English, in addition to their ethnic dialects. *See also* RACIAL, ETHNIC, AND RELIGIOUS TERMS.

both . . . and
See CORRELATIVE CONJUNCTIONS.

Brackets
A set of punctuation marks used inside quotations to enclose words that have been added by the writer: *"Fourscore*

and seven [87] years ago. . . ." Brackets can also be used to correct a faulty quotation*: "At about 6:00 [7:23 P.M. according to other witnesses] the night of the murder. . . ."* When quoting material that does not fit properly into your text because of capitalization, you may use brackets to modify the capitalization to fit your own sentence: *As the main character said, "[i]t shall be done."* Do not confuse brackets with parentheses. *See also* PARENTHESES.

Brand name
See GENERIC TERM VS. TRADEMARK.

Brevity
See CONCISENESS.

British spelling
Many British words find their way into American writing. Technically speaking, British spellings are unacceptable in standard American English. Beware of words ending in *-our*, *-re, -ise,* and containing double *l*s. In the following examples, the first spellings are acceptable American English: *color/colour; honor/honour; behavior/behaviour; center/centre; traveling/travelling; analyzing/analysing;* and *realize/realise.*

Business letter
The format of a business letter can vary, but its essential elements are usually the same. Typically, the writer includes his or her address, phone number, and fax number; sometimes this information is provided on letterhead. If you do not use letterhead, be sure to write your name, address, phone number, and fax number at the top of the page. The date follows your name and address, following the order *month, date, year (August 8, 1988).* This line may be justified either to the right or left of the page. The next element of your business letter is the name, title, company name, and address of the person to whom you are writing. Under this,

write in an appropriate greeting *(Dear Ms. Whatsit)* followed by either a colon or comma. Note that a colon is considered more formal than a comma, because commas are generally used in friendly or casual correspondence. The body of your letter should consist of short paragraphs separated by double spaces. Do not indent paragraphs in business letters. The text of the letter must clearly state why you are writing. You may be insistent, as long as you are courteous, when demanding something you justifiably deserve. Be straightforward and objective. At the end of the letter, use an appropriate closing *(Sincerely, Very Truly Yours, Best Regards)*. Sign your full name and type or print it clearly after the signature. The following is an example of a standard business letter:

Nancy Mitchell
64 Lexington Drive
Nelville, NY 12222
(618) 935-3400

October 4, 1996

Customer Service Representative
Blossom Magazine
102 Palmer Way
Washington, DC 21112

Dear Customer Service Representative:

I am writing to inquire about my subscription to Blossom Magazine. My subscription number is 1020-4387-2411Z. I signed up for a one-year subscription of Blossom last December and have thoroughly enjoyed the publication every month since then.

However, in the past two months, I have been bombarded with resubscription forms, letters, and calls from customer service representatives asking me to renew my subscription "before it's too late." Worried that I might miss a "special offer" for the $21.95 rate, I ordered another year's subscription from one of the telephone solicitors. The name of the person who assisted me on the phone was Steve. He assured me that I would not begin receiving my new subscription until my current one ran out in December. I was surprised to see two copies of this month's Blossom in my mailbox yesterday.

I would appreciate your help in getting this matter straightened out. I do not want to get two copies of each issue from now until December. I would like to resubscribe, but not until December.

Furthermore, I am wondering why the new subscriber rate is now "specially priced" at $19.95. I was informed by Steve that the $21.95 rate was a very good offer and that I would be saving money at that rate. Will you please change the billing amount of my new subscription to this lower price?

Thank you for your prompt attention to this matter.

Sincerely,

[INSERT SIGNATURE]

Nancy Mitchell

A letter of resignation often seems a monstrous task. If you find it necessary to write one, treat it as a business letter. For the body paragraph the following is acceptable:

I am writing this letter because I have decided to terminate my employment at Smith Company, Inc. My last day of work will be [two weeks from the date of the letter]. Thank you for the opportunity to work at this office, and good luck in the future.

See also RÉSUMÉS AND COVER LETTERS.

C

Cadence

The sound of a piece of writing, as if it were being read aloud. It is important to vary the length of your sentences to avoid monotony. Too many short sentences strung together can sound naïve and ineffective: *It was raining. The rain was strong. The wind was gusty. The window panes rattled. The dog howled.* In the same manner, long sentences of uniform construction can also sound unpolished: *We explored the abandoned woods near the old farmhouse; then we realized that the house had been abandoned as well. We broke the window to enter the house; it was clear that nothing in there had been touched for years.* Good writing consists of various types of sentences: long, short, rhyming, descriptive, repetitive, active, passive, etc. You can monitor the cadence of your writing by reading the words to yourself and assessing the interest level of each sentence, especially as compared to the sentences before and after it. Building your vocabulary is another excellent way to vary the cadences of your writing.

can

See MAY VS. CAN.

Capitalization

Always capitalize the first word of a sentence. Capitalize proper nouns *(New Jersey, Lake Tahoe)* including names for the deity *(God, Buddha)*, months *(June)*, days of the week *(Tuesday)*, organizations and companies *(Johnson & Johnson, Students Against Drunk Driving)*, publications and documents *(the New York Times, the Kama Sutra)*, and nations *(Canada)*. Capitalize titles when they are part of a proper name, but not when used alone *(District Attorney Smith, the district attorney)*. In titles and subtitles, capitalize the first, last, and important words *(The Land of the Free, Ten Days to a Slimmer Waist)*. Do not capitalize directions *(north, east)* or seasons *(winter)*. Never capitalize words in running text just to stress their importance.

Case: Subjective, objective, possessive

Nouns and pronouns take different cases depending on the tense and context of the sentence. Every noun and pronoun that is the subject of a sentence (doing the action described) takes the subjective case: *I, you, he, she, it, we, you, they, who (I am; They swim)*. Pronouns that occur in the objective case (receiving the action described) are: *me, you, him, her, it, us, them, whom (The dog bit him; Give the ball to me)*. Pronouns in the possessive case are: *my, mine, your, yours, his, her, hers, its, our, ours, their, theirs, whose (This is your life; The package is for whom?)*. It is essential to know the differences among the three cases, and to use each properly.

Casual tone

See FORMAL VS. INFORMAL.

Charts

See TABLES AND CHARTS.

Circumlocution

Literally, this means "talking in circles." Writers should avoid this and get directly to the point. Using redundant language (also known as "beating around the bush") is not acceptable in good writing. Avoid wordiness, clichés, and empty filler phrases such as *in this particular situation, in a manner of speaking, something or other, in terms of this type of thing,* etc. Your readers will appreciate your direct approach to the point that you are trying to make. Reread, revise, and rewrite your work. As you review what you have written, you will be better able to identify your own tendency to talk in circles. *See also* CONCISENESS; DRAFTS; *and* REDUNDANCY.

Citation

Whenever you borrow an idea, you must attribute credit for ideas, facts, illustrations, summaries, or words that are not your own. Parenthetical citations occur within your text as a way to give credit for a quote or idea without interrupting the flow of your writing. A bibliography or list of works cited must appear at the end of the document, comprehensively listing every work cited parenthetically or implicitly. Although styles of parenthetical citation vary, the information usually includes the name of the author or editor, the year of publication, and the page number. Here are some examples:

Author not mentioned in the text:
There are several approaches to child care (Spock, 1972, p. 3).

Author mentioned in the text:
In his first collection of essays, Dr. Ouest (1983, p. 42) proposes that there are three schools of modern historical thought.

An anonymous author:
The article mentioned by the speaker ("Let's Go Crazy," 1995) has been published in at least three union journals.

See also BIBLIOGRAPHY; FOOTNOTE; *and* QUOTATIONS.

Clarity

All writing benefits from clear expression. This means defined agruments, easy-to-follow sentence structure, smooth paragraph transitions, and proper word choice. If you are using examples to support an argument or to illustrate a point, make sure that you explain how the examples relate to your idea. Watch out for dangling modifiers and misplaced phrases that may confuse your reader. If you are explaining an abstract notion or attempting to make your readers understand a difficult point, keep your sentences short and descriptive. Reread your work often and always check to see if one idea flows logically into the next. If it doesn't, you need transitions and explanations to achieve clarity. *See also* CONCISENESS; TRANSITIONAL PHRASE; *and* TRANSITIONAL SENTENCE.

Cliché

An overused expression devoid of fresh meaning. Most clichés started out as fun, interesting phrases but have become dull and annoying because of excessive repetition. Some examples: *better late than never; beyond all expectation; like a bull in a china shop; crystal clear: like there's no tomorrow; like you wouldn't believe; thin as a rail; sharp as a needle; stuck like glue*. Use you own creative expressions to convey meaning; don't rely on the words of other people. If you find yourself using an expression already familiar to you, rephrase your sentence.

Collective noun

A word that refers to a group of people or things: *audience* is a single word that names several people; a *pod* of whales and a *bushel* of apples likewise are terms that represent many objects. According to standard American English, collective nouns are singular and agree with singular verbs: *The audience is laughing at the joke; A pod of whales was swimming near the galleon; A bushel of apples was collected from the orchard.*

Some collective nouns can be used in the singular or plural, depending on context:

An assortment of nuts was delivered to the office; An assortment of nuts—pecans, walnuts, and cashews—were shipped to Vermont. See also AGREEMENT; NOUN.

Colloquial language

Informal or everyday speech. Colloquialisms are most commonly used when grammatically correct language seems stuffy and a more conversational tone is desired. Many colloquial words and expressions are acceptable in some forms of writing (such as vignettes and opinion pieces) but not always in others (such as works of academic scholarship). Examples of colloquial language: *freebie; bum steer; TV.*

Colon

The colon has two general uses. The most common is to indicate a main idea: *This is the candidate's point: Let's give the corporate constituency a run for its money. The following ingredients were used in the recipe: watercress, leeks, and dill.* Note that a capital letter follows the colon if the idea that follows it is a complete sentence. Otherwise, the use of the lowercase prevails.

The second general use is to balance or compare two similar ideas, especially in cases where the second point clarifies or expands the first: *Many considered him obstinate: He refused to participate in the sit-in even after it became apparent that his absence would weaken their cause.*

Comma

The comma has many uses, the most basic of which is to separate two or more elements in a list, such as nouns or phrases: *We bought peaches, plums, and bananas; See no evil, hear no evil, speak no evil.* It should be noted that some book, newspaper, and magazine publishers avoid the second comma—known as a serial comma—in lists of three. The decision about whether to use the serial comma or not mostly depends on company style, although sometimes you may be allowed to follow your personal preference. Whether you use it or not, once you've made the choice, be consistent: All lists should either contain or not contain the last comma in a series.

Commas are also used to separate the following sentence elements.

Introductory Clauses:

Longer clauses such as prepositional, participial, or infinitive phrases that begin sentences are frequently separated by a comma: *It was the best of times, it was the worst of times; After several cutbacks in social programs, the community began to deteriorate.* What constitutes "longer" is often a matter of personal judgment, and some writers feel comfortable setting all introductory phrases off by a comma: *At the end, there will be a panel discussion.* Be sure to consistently adhere to whatever decisions you make about which phrases to set off.

Quoted speech:

Phrases in which someone is quoted are commonly set off with commas as well as quotation marks: *"Let's go to the beach," said Michelle; The boy asked, "May I pet the hamster?"* These commas appear within the quotes if the speaker follows the quotation marks.

Longer quotations can also be introduced by a comma, even though quotation marks do not generally appear around the quoted speech: *The philosopher Hegel remarked,*

> *What experience and history teach us is this—that people and governments have never learned anything from history, or acted on principles deduced from it. . . .*

He then commented further on the state of society.

The comma following the word *remarked* could also be a colon or omitted altogether. Again, once you have made a decision, the most important thing is to stick to it throughout your writing.

Direct address:

Names of people directly addressed in a sentence are usually set off with commas: *Donald, I thought I told you; I'm afraid, Susan, that you did not.*

Place names:

The elements of a location, such as addresses and other place names, are separated with commas: *Butte, Montana; Washington, D.C.; Surrey Road, Stratford-upon-Avon, England.*

Parenthetical phrases:

While insignificant or interjected words inserted in a sentence are best placed in parentheses, certain short phrases are commonly separated by commas: *As you know, there's going to be a lot of sightseeing; I don't know how to say this, but I'm afraid I've decided to move on; In my opinion, his performance is not up to par.*

Appositives:

Words that have equivalent meaning and stand together without connecting words are in apposition. Such words are commonly set off by commas: *The former mayor of Peekskill, George Pataki, will make a brief speech.*

Dates:

Commas are used to divide the month, day, and/or year of a date: *April 18, 1972.*

Numbers:

It is accepted in standard American usage to place commas in numbers greater than 999: *1,000; $4,655,000.00.* Note that commas are not used in dates: *(1967),* but are used when counting years *(1,967 years ago).*

Titles:

Titles following people's names are frequently set off by commas: *George Irwin, Esq.; Andrew Brown, Sr.; Estelle Brady, M.D., F.A.C.P.* Numerals following names, as well as titles preceding names, do not require commas: *Catherine II; Dr. Jane Williams.*

Clarity:

It is sometimes useful to insert a comma for the sake of clearness, even if you are not required to do so by any rule.

RIGHT: *They caught on, in great numbers, and began flooding the doors of the shop.* Although no rule requires the insertion of the first comma, it may help clarify the meaning of the sentence for some readers. The sentence would probably be sufficient without the first comma; the second one is required. It is sometimes best to rewrite such sentences altogether.

Also, bear in mind that is not a good idea to add commas just to be on the safe side, as this frequently causes more confusion. WRONG: *The donkey, and the rooster were waiting by the barn door; Give this, to Kathy and tell her to see me; Joe stated, that this is the new procedure.* In these examples, there is no need for a comma; the addition of one creates confusion.

Comparative

Comparative forms demonstrate the margin of difference between two or more items. The comparative usually involves the use of an auxiliary word such as *more,* or the comparative or superlative forms of words *(stronger, strongest).*

Some irregular comparatives follow different patterns: *bad, worse, worst.* It is best to memorize these patterns and not add comparative elements to such words. WRONG: *more worse.* Take note of the following irregular patterns: *good, better, best; more* and *most* for use with *many, much* and *some; little,: less, least* when indicating quantity; and *littler, littlest* when indicating size.

Also note that when more than two things or people are compared, superlatives are required: *The hare is faster than the tortoise; Of all the animals, the hare is the fastest runner.* WRONG: *The hare is the fastest of the two.*

Be sure to complete all comparisons. WRONG: *The hare is faster.* RIGHT: *The hare is faster than the tortoise is.* In the right context, the first example could be admissible, but only if information in preceding sentences has made it completely clear who or what is being compared. *See also* SUPERLATIVE.

compare to vs. compare with

Use *compare with* when saying one thing is like something else: *Anne compared her findings with Tony's.* Use *compare to* for comparisons of similarities and differences: *This garden does not compare with the great gardens of the south of France.*

Complaint, letter of

See ANGER; BUSINESS LETTER.

Compound word

A word comprised of two or more elements: *attorney general, bus driver,* and *nonproliferation pact* are all compound words. There is often confusion surrounding the composition of compound words—whether they should be hyphenated *(city-state, hearing impaired),* be run together *(milkshake),* or remain two separate words *(orange juice).* Some compound words, such as *carjacking,* have made a transition from two words to one as they become more common. When you are in doubt about the configuration of a compound word, it is best to consult a dictionary. *See also* **Style Quick-Finder.**

Conciseness

In all forms of writing, strive to present your ideas in clear, precise language. Conciseness starts with choosing the right words—those that most accurately convey your ideas. Once you have selected which words you will use, you need to connect them in clear, succinct sentences before you can set about the task of making clear paragraphs or clear reports. Verbose or rambling language can hinder reader comprehension and make the intent of your writing incoherent. The following example demonstrates excessive language:

> When we finally get to the point about seventeenth century nobility, we can begin to see the thematic direction in which the playwright may having been headed, i.e., the stalwarted attempts of exceptionally talented members of the bourgeoisie to rise in the ranks of nobility in seventeenth century France as parallel to the struggle between Louis XV and a small number of his intimates in their dealings with Russia; however, whatever points he is presumably trying to emboss on the collective subconscious of the audience, (which, incidentally, are hampered by dense highly stylized dialogue), are lost as we swiftly delve into the subplot of Miranda's quixotic relationship with the Count.

This sentence is clumsily constructed and riddled with grammatical errors. The ideas the author is attempting to put across are buried in the murky language. To avoid imprecise and meandering prose, make sure you know what it is you want to say before you put it down on paper. That way, when you are choosing words, you can do so with confidence. In addition, be on the lookout for misplaced modifiers, dangling prepositions, awkward transitions and other errors that may hinder the conciseness of your prose.

Condolence, letter of

When sending a letter of sympathy to someone who has suffered a loss, the fact that you are writing is often more important than what you write. However, there are a few guidelines you should heed in order to avoid writing anything that might be viewed as inappropriate or offensive by the person receiving the letter. For instance, if you have not suffered a similar loss, it is generally not a good idea to be empathetic in tone: *I know exactly how you feel.* Don't radiate false emotion. If a loss hasn't deeply affected you, don't write that it has; you can be honest in your sympathy without being profoundly influenced by the loss yourself. Also, don't offer to help unless you can honestly follow through.

Letters of condolence should be personal in nature; their contents should be tailored to the relationship between the sender and the receiver. Above all, aim to write with tact and sincerity. The following is a sample letter of condolence:

Dear Mavis:

I was sorry to hear of Ernie's passing. I have fond memories of him and will miss him dearly. I know the two of you had a special relationship and that he loved you very much. Please let me know if there is anything I can do for you during this time.

With sympathy,

Olivia

Confused words

The following is a list of words that are commonly confused:

advice/advise	emigrant/immigrant
affect/effect	imply/infer
allusion/illusion	lay/lie
all ready/already	lead/led
all right/alright	lend/loan
all together/altogether	loose/lose
anybody/any body	maybe/may be
anymore/any more	proceed/precede
assure/ensure/insure	raise/rise
anyone/any one	stationary/stationery

cite/sight/site	*than/then*
compose/comprise	*their/there/they're*
connotation/denotation	*your/you're*
elicit/illicit	

Use extra caution when using these words, which may look similar but have different meanings. When in doubt, check a dictionary to be sure you've chosen the correct word. *See also* HOMONYMS; HOMOPHONES; SYNONYMS; *and* **Style Quick-Finder.**

Connective
See TRANSITIONAL PHRASE; TRANSITIONAL SENTENCE.

Consistency
When preparing any kind of writing—a book manuscript, an essay, a term paper, etc.—it is crucial that you review the material several times to make sure that styles have been ridigly followed globally. Consistency within a piece of writing optimizes clarity for the reader and helps prevent miscommunication. For example, if a serial comma (the third comma in a list) appears in chapters one through six of a book, it should also be used in seven through the end. If a noun is capitalized in some places in a manuscript and lowercased in another, the reader might incorrectly interpret that to mean that you are referring to two separate items.

Consistency may also refer to the unity of ideas within a work. Writers must be careful of sentences or details that read as contradictory or misleading based on information presented earlier in the work. If you state that there were six baseball players at a party, but then proceed to list only four, readers will be confused and may even doubt future facts that you present. Edit and proofread your work thoroughly to avoud such problems. *See also* AGREEMENT.

Context
The subject matter, circumstances, settings, tone and other elements that make up the framework of a piece of writing.

Continuity

The "flow" of a piece of writing. In most cases, the paragraph will be the building block of whatever piece you are working on. Each paragraph should relate to the preceding and following ones in a meaningful way. The first and last sentences of each paragraph should act as bridges or transitions, and should support continuity. The following example shows how ideas presented are logically connected.

An eclipse occurs when a celestial body produces a shadow that makes another celestial body seem to disappear. A lunar eclipse occurs when the sun, Earth, and moon are aligned so that the moon casts a shadow on the earth. Each of the celestial bodies is constantly in motion, so the eclipse may not be absolute; also, it is rare for eclipses to last more than a few minutes. The eclipse may be partial or total.

A total eclipse of the sun occurs when the alignment of the sun, Earth, and moon is such that the dark, cone-shaped part of the moon's shadow reaches Earth and all the light of the sun is blocked because of the moon's position.

Contraction

Abbreviated forms of two words may be used in informal speech and writing. Some examples of contractions are: *I'm* (I am); *isn't* (is not); *we've* (we have). Contractions listed in dictionaries are acceptable, but they should be restricted to informal texts where they reflect the mode in which a phrase commonly appears in speech or writing. One should be consistent when using contractions, and use them sparingly.

Correlative conjunctions

Either/or, both/and, and *not only/but also* are all examples of correlative conjunctions—pairs of parallel expressions. One common mistake when writing is to mismatch these expressions grammatically. WRONG: *The engine will either die or the fan belt will stop working.* The verb *die* is mismatched with the clause *the fan belt will stop working.* Rearranging the sentence creates a parallel structure: RIGHT: *Either the en-*

gine will die or the fan belt will stop working. *See also* PAR-
ALLEL STRUCTURE.

Cover letter
See RÉSUMÉS AND COVER LETTERS.

Dangling modifier
A descriptive or modifying element placed in such a way as
to modify the wrong term or "dangle" in the sentence without
clearly modifying anything. The following examples contain
dangling modifiers: *Poor and hungry, the cup of soup seemed
a depressing choice; Recently diagnosed with terminal cancer, John and his son moved to the Adirondacks; Dedicated to
helping needy children, her first mission to Cambodia was
very fulfilling.*

In the first example, the soup seems poor and hungry,
when what is meant is: *To the poor and hungry individual,
the cup of soup seemed a depressing choice.* In the second
example, the modifier applies only to the first part of a compound sentence. It should rearranged for clarity: *Recently
diagnosed with terminal cancer, John moved to the Adirondacks with his son.* The last example contains a modifier that
is sloppily attached to a possessive, making it sound as if *her
first mission* is *dedicated to helping needy children.* The sentence can be correctly reworded: *She had dedicated her life
to helping needy children, and her first mission to Cambodia
was fulfilling.*

Dashes
The dash, or em dash (—) is most frequently used to separate parts of a sentence that are basically equivalent but lack

conjunctions: *Our favorite spectator sport—cricket—is more popular in Europe than in America.* The pair of dashes here replace the words *that is.* Em dashes can also join two clauses: *Don't cry—it's only a trivial mistake.*

The smaller en dash (–) is useful in compound nouns in which at least one of the elements is two words: *The Cleveland Indians–Atlanta Braves series.* Also, ranges of numbers are commonly separated by the en dash: *From 1948–1963, the Yankees were the dominant team in baseball. See also* HYPHEN.

Dates

There are several systems for expressing dates in writing. Which system you use in your writing depends on your audience.

The most commonly used system is *month, day, year.* The full name of the month comes before the number of the day, a comma follows, and then comes the number of the year: *March 1, 1996.* The number of the year is generally followed by a comma if the sentence continues; *On March 1, 1996, the contract took effect.*

If the day of the week is specified in this style, it can come before the date and is followed by a comma: *Sunday, March 17, 1996.* When the day of the week follows the date, it is preceded by a comma and usually adds an article, as the following day is seen as an afterthought or interjection: *March 17, 1996, a Sunday.* Commas are not needed if the month and year alone are recorded: *It occurred in March 1996.*

In formal English, it is common to spell out dates in one of these systems. However, it is becoming more acceptable to express dates in numbers alone using dashes (-) or slashes (/): *3-17-96* or *3/17/96.*

Degree of comparison

See COMPARATIVE.

Dependent clause

A clause that cannot stand on its own as a complete sentence: *When the weather breaks, we will go fishing. When the weather breaks* is a fragment or dependent clause that has no meaning by itself. The core of the clause *(the weather breaks)* could be a sentence by itself, but the addition of the conjunction *when* makes the clause dependent.

Diagonal

See SLASH.

Dialect

A regional variation in speech. Writing dialect can be tricky, especially, if you do not have a thorough familiarity with the speech patterns in question. Mark Twain began his novel *The Adventures of Huckleberry Finn* with a note to his readers:

> *In this book, a number of dialects are used, to wit: the Missouri Negro dialect; the extremest form of the backwoods Southwestern dialect; the ordinary "Pike County" dialect; and four modified varieties of this last. The shadings have not been done in a haphazard fashion, or by guesswork; but painstakingly, and with the trustworthy guidance and support of personal familiarity with these several forms of speech.*

> *I make this explanation for the reason that without it many readers would suppose that all these characters were trying to talk alike and not succeeding.*

Without authenticity born of hard work and personal experience, dialects can result in sloppy stereotyping. Don't attempt to capture dialect in writing unless you are highly familiar with it. *See also* COLLOQUIAL LANGUAGE.

Dialogue

The recording of others' speech in writing is called dialogue. Quotation marks are usually used to indicate directly recorded speech: *"Let's go,"* he said.

Directly quoted speech can also be indented and made into

a block quotation to indicate that the words of someone other than the author are being related: *The newscaster said,*

> *A plane crash in the Detroit area has occurred within the last two hours. EMS workers are struggling to remove survivors from the tangle of debris, but so far few have been found. Flight 107 from Washington, D.C., was scheduled to arrive in Detroit this morning when it reportedly fell out of the sky and crashed in a field in a nearby suburb. We will keep you updated on this tragic story throughout the night as more information comes in.*

> *The news magazine ended shortly thereafter.*

Direct speech within dialogue is usually placed in single quotes: " *'I'm going to sleep,' he announced.*" See also GO VS. SAY.

Diction

The choice and use of words. *See also* CLARITY.

different from vs. different than

The standard American usage is *different from: Eastwood's movies are different from classic Westerns in many subtle ways.* There are some exceptions: *I am different than I used to be. From* takes a direct object, so in order to use *from* in this case, the sentence must be reconstructed: *I am different from what I used to be.*

Digression

A digression is a deviation from a train of thought. In writing, digressions can serve many purposes, such as building suspense or preparing a reader for a challenging argument. Most of the time, however, digressions serve no purpose, and can distract readers.

Direct quotation

See QUOTATION.

Disability terms

See POLITICAL CORRECTNESS.

Discourse

Formal, orderly, and often extended expression of thought on an idea or ideas.

disinterested vs. *uninterested*

Disinterested means objective or impartial: *We will have a disinterested arbiter settle the dispute. Uninterested* means not interested: *I am uninterested in hearing your excuse.*

Documentation

See BIBLIOGRAPHY; CITATION; *and* FOOTNOTE.

Double negative

It is unacceptable in standard American usage to include more than one negative word in a sentence, clause or verb phrase. WRONG: *I've never done nothing that would cause harm.* RIGHT: *I've never done anything that would cause harm.* Having double or multiple negatives is a common error, particularly when a sentence is long, allowing the early negation of an element to be forgotten later on. Careful proof-reading of your work will ensure that there are no double or multiple negatives in your writing.

Drafts

Nearly every piece of writing must go through several revisions before being turned in. The process of creating these successive drafts includes reviewing them for general content, style, and format, as well as correcting grammar, spelling, and syntax in later drafts. After a clean first draft is completed, it is highly recommended that the writer present the pages to a friend or colleague for a quick review prior to submission. The final draft of any manuscript must be proofread one last time to ensure that final corrections have been entered properly and that no typos or errors have been overlooked.

due to vs. *because*

See BECAUSE VS. DUE TO.

each vs. *every*

Each can be used as a pronoun: *Each went to the museum.*
It can also be used as an adjective: *Each basket contains eggs.*
Each represents the individual units of a whole: *each of the
Green Berets.* However, *every* represents the whole itself:
every Green Beret. In the *Green Beret* examples, *each* is act-
ing as a pronoun, *every* an adjective.

When *each* modifies a singular noun, the following verb
and pronouns are singular: *Each man takes off his hat.* When
each modifies a plural noun or pronoun and comes before the
verb, the verb and pronouns are plural: *They each take their
hats off.* When *each* acts a pronoun, it is typically singular:
each takes off his hat.

When *each* refers to two or more singular words, or when a
plural word comes between *each* and the verb, the number of
the verb is optional: *each of the men is* or *each of the men are.*

Editing

See DRAFTS.

e.g. vs. *i.e.*

E.g. is an abbreviation standing for the Latin term *exempli
gratia* ("for example"). It is most frequently used in academic
or other formal documents: *Many studies of human sexuality,
e.g., the Kinsey study, were conducted after the early 1950s.*
When writing in more informal styles, it is better to stick with
for example.

E.g. is often mistakenly used when *i.e.,* an abbreviation for
the Latin term *id est* ("that is") is intended. *I.e.* is commonly
used to draw attention to something: *Founded in 1895, one of
the few institutions with a collection of literature on the
Atomic Energy Commission, i.e., the Carnegie Library, began
acquiring various government publications.* However, unless

lack of space is a consideration, it is more acceptable to use the English *that is*.

either . . . or
See CORRELATIVE CONJUNCTION.

Ellipsis
The omission of text for any reason is called an *ellipsis* (plural: *ellipses*). It is normally indicated by three consecutive periods: *Her first novel is filled with literary gems . . . an important landmark in the genre.* If the ellipsis occurs at the end of a sentence, a fourth period is added to indicate the end of the sentence. This is often used when an ellipsis refers to a thought that is left incomplete: *That is a completely different situation. . . .* Four ellipsis points also are used between sentences in large blocks of quotations when other sentences have been deleted.

Ellipses that come before other parts of sentences can be followed by other punctuation: *The three most important things to remember are the inclusion of the graph, the mention of a possible formation of a subsidiary company . . . , and the presentation of the annual earnings chart.*

Since ellipses represent the omission of text or the lack of completed thought, they can present the reader with gaps in information. Consequently, ellipses should be carefully used to preserve the meaning of a quoted source and the full intent of a shortened sentence.

E-mail
An abbreviation for *electronic mail,* a computerized communication system with an extensive network. *See also* NETIQUETTE.

Em dash
See DASH.

Emphasis
See ITALICS.

En dash
See DASH.

Endnote
See DOCUMENTATION.

equally as
Equally and *as* have the same meaning, so the combination *equally as* is redundant. WRONG: *He feels equally as strongly about the need for a teen center.* RIGHT: *He and you feel equally strongly about the need for a teen center.* Or: *He feels as strongly as you about the need for a teen center.*

Essay
When attempting to write an essay (a composition dealing with its subject from a personal point of view), you should follow some basic guidelines. First, make sure you have a clear idea of what it is you want to convey. What is the purpose and central idea you want to put across? Who is your audience? What tone is most appropriate to the subject matter? Next, select a title that reflects that tone and subject matter.

When writing the essay, pay close attention to structure. Is the essay unified and coherent? Do all of the paragraphs contribute to the main topic? Make sure that there is adequate information to back up your central thesis, along with enough examples and/or reasons to support each of your ideas. The opening paragraph should reflect the purpose of the essay, and the conclusion should wrap your ideas up neatly and provide a sense of closure.

When you have created a first draft, read it over carefully to make sure there is an overall shape to it, that your thoughts are well organized and clearly presented, and that there are no grammatical errors. *See also* DRAFTS.

Etc.
The abbreviation of the Latin term *et cetera* meaning "and so on." This is an overused abbreviation, often communicat-

ing little to your audience other than the fact that you probably haven't given enough thought to what you want to say and are merely filling in the gaps. Therefore, use *etc.* sparingly. When you see it creeping into your writing in several places, regard it as a sign that you need to go back and rethink, augment, and amend what you are saying.

Ethnic terms
See RACIAL, ETHNIC, AND RELIGIOUS TERMS.

Euphemism
A euphemism is a "polite" way of expressing something considered unpleasant, offensive or in bad taste. Too often, overcompensation has rendered the euphemism more offensive than the phrase it was intended to replace. If you announce at a meeting that your boss has *gone to the litter box,* it may be viewed by some people as disrespectful. In some cases, a different euphemism may be more appropriate: *She went to the ladies' room.* If you need to use a euphemism, choose it carefully.

every
See EACH VS. EVERY.

Exclamatory sentence
An exclamatory sentence, by definition, is followed by an exclamation point. If a sentence does not require an exclamation point, then it is not an exclamatory sentence. Examples of exclamatory sentences: *Can you believe the nerve of that waiter! Look at the speed of that fastball! My, that dog is huge!*

Expletive
There are two meanings for this word: *bland introductory word* and *strong language.* Grammatical expletives are weak constructions used to introduce sentences. These expletives begin with *it* or *there* and are followed by forms of *be: There*

were ten puppies. Such constructions offer some emphasis because they change the most common sentence order, but the device is often overused by writers. Consequently, there is usually little emphasis to be gained from such sentences, which should probably be revised.

The other type of explectives, or words that go beyond the boundaries of good taste (good taste being determined by the audience you are writing for), can add zest and humor to your writing, but should be used with great caution, as it is often hard to predict whether the use of expletives will offend someone. When in doubt, leave them out.

Expository writing

Writing that is primarily explanatory in nature. Almost all topics are suitable for expository writing, from how to make a birdhouse to major trends in consumer spending. Expository writing is encountered everywhere: newspapers, magazines, textbooks. In short, anything that explains something to readers is considered exposition. *See also* ESSAY.

farther vs. *further*

The formal distinction between these two words is blurred but should be observed in standard writing. Use *farther* to refer to distance: *I think the house is farther up the road.* Use *further* to refer to degree or time: *We realized the project could go no further.*

Faulty parallelism

See PARALLEL STRUCTURE.

feel bad vs. *feel badly*

Bad is an adjective; *badly* is an adverb: *I feel bad that you're not coming to Scotland; This sweater feels badly against my skin.*

Feminine

See GENDER; SEXIST LANGUAGE.

few vs. *several*

See SEVERAL VS. A FEW.

fewer vs. *less*

The difference between these two words is significant but often disregarded. By preserving the distinction between them, you will add precision and lucidity to your writing. *Fewer* refers to things that are easily counted one by one, such as people or most common objects: *There are fewer tables available for dining than I expected. Less* is used with things that are not easily counted: *There is less information in the file than I thought.*

Figurative language

Speech or writing that is analogous in sense, as opposed to literal: *sidesplitting humor; tearing one's hair out; scared to death.* See also LITERALLY.

First person

See POINT OF VIEW.

Focus

Every piece of writing must have a topic that holds the entire piece together. When you are writing an essay, for example, you should establish the focus of the work prior to getting started. Often, a teacher's assignment itself provides the initial focus of a project, although in many cases you will be responsible for deciding on your topic. In either event, you must ensure that every paragraph within the essay itself is concerned primarily with the topic, or else the teacher will accuse you of having an "unfocused" work. When the first draft of a work is completed, always take a special read through it to make sure that there are no paragraphs that stray from the main topic. *See also* DRAFTS.

Footnote

A note of reference, explanation, or comment usually placed below the text on a printed page. Following are some guidelines for using footnotes in your writing.

Numbering:

Use a consistent system of numbering. In most writing, footnotes are numbered consecutively throughout a chapter. In scientific and reference writing, they are typically numbered by page.

Authors' names:

Authors' first names are usually spelled out. When two authors have the same last name, spell the name out twice. For works by three or more authors, list all the authors or use *et al.* ("and others").

Titles of publications:

Titles should be represented exactly as they appeared in the original work, including original punctuation between titles and subtitles.

Repeated references:

Ibid., op. cit., and *loc. cit.* can be used for footnote references that appear in whole or part within the same chapter. *Ibid.,* or "in the same place," is substituted for the author and title and any additional publishing data identical to those in the preceding footnote. *Op. cit.,* or "in the work cited," can be substituted for the title and publishing data of a work of the same author cited earlier but not in the immediately preceding footnote. When you use *op. cit.,* the original footnote must contain the author's name. *Loc. cit.,* or "in the place cited," is commonly used instead of *op. cit.* when the page numbers referred to are identical.

Sample footnote:
[1]James T. Kirk. *My Years as Captain* (New York: Cyberspace Publishing Co., 1996), pp. 85–88.

Note the slight differences between how information is presented in a footnote and in a bibliographic citation. *See also* BIBLIOGRAPHY.

Foreign terms

It is standard to use roman type for words that have been assimilated into the English language and italics for words that haven't. Because the degree of assimilation may vary from one context to another, check a dictionary when in doubt as to whether you should use roman type or italics. Examples of foreign terms that typically require italics are: *haute couture, Gemütlichkeit,* and *pro tempore.*

Formal vs. informal language

Clearly expressing yourself depends on what words you choose and how you employ them in your writing. Sometimes, a situation may call for formal language (standard American language), informal language (including slang colloquialisms, euphemisms, and/or expletives), or a combination of both. The selections you make should be appropriate to the situation— your subject, intent, and audience. You should use formal language in formal academic and professional or business writing. Informal or a mix of formal and informal writing is usually more acceptable in personal letters and creative or opinion pieces. When in doubt about the appropriateness of certain language, it is better to err on the side of formality.

former vs. *latter*

Former refers to the first of two things, *latter* to the second: I *like both mimosas and martinis, the former at brunch and the latter at cocktail hour.* To refer to the first or last named thing when naming three or more things, use *first* and *last*: I *like mimosas, screwdrivers, and martinis, but the last is inappropriate for a traditional brunch.*

Form of address

Forms of address are also known as titles: *Ms.; Mrs.; Miss; Mr.; Dr.; Sir; Madam; Professor; King*. When addressing a letter, make sure you are using the proper form of address. If you need to write to a J. Silman, and are not certain whether this is a man or a woman, do not assume it is *Mr.* Silman. Call and find out or, if necessary, resort to *To Whom It May Concern*. *See also* GENDER.

Fragment

See SENTENCE FRAGMENT.

further

See FARTHER VS. FURTHER.

Future tense

See TENSE: PAST, PRESENT, FUTURE.

G

Gender

Gender is a way of classifying pronouns or nouns, such as masculine, feminine, or neuter. The masculine pronouns are *he, him*, and *his*. Masculine nouns include: *man, boy, guy, bull*. Proper masculine nouns include men's and boys' names: *Jeremy, Joe, Mr. Bentley*. The feminine pronouns are *she, her,* and *hers*. Feminine nouns include: *woman, girl, cow*. Proper feminine nouns are all women's and girls' names: *Jane; Arianne; Ms. Clifton*. The neuter pronouns are *it* and *its*. Almost all regular nouns are neuter: *flag, hat, computer, one*. When using the indefinite pronoun *one*, you may use a feminine pronoun, a masculine pronoun, or a combination of the two: *One needs to choose whether to use <u>his</u> / <u>her</u> / <u>his or her</u> stage* *name in real life.* It is inappropriate to use a neuter pronoun *(it)* when referring to a person. Whichever pronoun you choose for sentences containing the subject *one,* avoid sexist language and be consistent in your usage. *See also* SEXIST LANGUAGE.

Generic term vs. trademark

Generic nouns refer to an entire category of products, while trademark names identify a particular brand of a product. Do not capitalize generic nouns. *Aluminum foil* is a generic noun; *Reynolds Wrap* is a trademark. It is advisable to avoid trademark names in your writing because some companies insist that you obtain permission to use their trade name. When a trade name loses its association with a specific brand and comes to refer to a general type of product, it has become generic. *Thermos* used to be a specific trademark item made by Thermos; now, *thermoses* are made by a number of manufacturers. Other examples of trademarked terms are: *Scotch tape,* and *Xerox.* Watch out for *Band-Aid* meaning adhesive bandage, *Coke* meaning cola, *Filofax* meaning address book, *Jell-O* meaning gelatin, *Kleenex* meaning tissue, *Q-Tips* meaning cotton swabs, *Walkman* meaning portable stereo, and *Liquid Paper* meaning correction fluid. *See also* **Style Quick-Finder.**

go vs. *say*

Go does not mean *say.* Spoken American English has almost come to accept the interchangeableness of the two verbs when describing dialogue: *"Let's go," I went. She went, "O.K., but I need to get my jacket."* The correct form of dialogue indication is to use the verb *say. "Let's go," I said. See also* DIALOGUE.

good vs. *well*

Good is an adjective; *well* is an adverb. *Good* modifies nouns: *the good man; the meal was good. Well* modifies verbs: *the dancer performed well; I am feeling well.* The confusion between the two arises with the verbs *look* and *feel*. *He looks good* means that he is attractive; *good* is modifying *he*. *He looks well* means that he appears healthy; *well* is modifying *looks*.

got vs. *gotten*

Past tense and past participle of the verb *get. Got* can be properly used in the phrase *have got (he has got the flu)*, but never by itself *(I got a cold)*. However, note that both *got* and *gotten* are inappropriate for formal writing. Substitute a more descriptive word when possible. *Lara has gotten better at skiing* can be easily rewritten as *Lara has become a better skier*.

Grammar

Grammar is a set of rules that governs the structure of language. It is concerned with the functions and relationships of words in sentences. Proper grammar, in addition to accurate usage, contributes to a writer's ability to create meaningful, persuasive, and engaging prose.

H

had better

See BETTER VS. HAD BETTER.

Haughtiness

A tone contempt or disdain for the reader or audience. There is no reason to take a deliberately haughty tone in your writing. Even if you are attempting to sound authoritative or masterful, haughtiness comes across as vicious, spiteful, and condescending. Don't alienate your readers.

he or *she*

See GENDER; POLITICAL CORRECTNESS; *and* PRONOUN.

herself
See REFLEXIVE PRONOUN.

himself
See REFLEXIVE PRONOUN.

Hispanic
A descendant of any of the Spanish-speaking countries of Central or South America, Mexico, or the Caribbean. This is an adjective, not a noun. Refer to *Hispanic people*, not *Hispanics*. *See also* RACIAL, ETHNIC, *and* RELIGIOUS TERMS.

Homonyms
Words that are spelled and pronounced the same, but have different meanings: *quick* (cut to the quick) and *quick* (speedy); *quail* (the bird) and *quail* (to falter). Be careful with the context of words that have different meanings. *See also* CONFUSED WORDS; **Style Quick-Finder.**

Homophones
Words that are pronounced the same, but have different spellings and meanings: *to, two, too*; *allowed, aloud; dual, duel*. Be sure you use the correct spelling and meaning. *See also* CONFUSED WORDS; **Style Quick-Finder.**

hopefully
An adverb meaning "with hope.": *I awaited the verdict hopefully*. In recent usage, hopefully has become a modifier meaning "one hopes": *Hopefully, the jury will find me innocent.* Using *hopefully* as a modifier is idiomatic and should be avoided in formal writing. If you write *Sam will hopefully arrive on the 3:00 train*, you are implying that when Sam arrives at 3:00, she will be full of hope.

however
A conjunction meaning "although". When used after a semicolon, *however* almost always takes a comma before the

rest of the sentence: *We would love to stay; however, it is past Brian's bedtime. However* is a very useful transition; when used at the beginning of a paragraph or a sentence, it signifies an opposing view or reaction. *See also* TRANSITIONAL PHRASE; TRANSITIONAL SENTENCE.

Hung paragraph

An indented paragraph consisting of more than three sentences of quoted material; also referred to as "setting off" a paragraph. When separating a hung paragraph, indent more than the usual ten-space tab (use two tabs or twenty spaces), use single-space, and do not use quotation marks. Example:

> *The best description of the author's family life begins with the discussion of her older sister when they were young:*
>
> > *Nan was a bully, but she was the type of tough kid you wanted to mimic. Pushy, boisterous, feisty: her defiance inspired me to leave my complacence and fight for what I needed. This included freedom and independence, but it also meant confronting the problems that had boiled to the surface at home.* (p. 61)

Note the page number cited at the end of the hung paragraph. Also, it is conventional to introduce the quotation with a brief description of what follows (in this example, " . . . when they were young:"). *See also* BIBLIOGRAPHY; CITATION; FOOTNOTE; *and* QUOTATION.

Hyperbole

Exaggeration or theatricality. Hyperbole can be a useful writing tool when used sparingly and discerningly. It is found mostly in fiction creative prose writing, and advertising: *The diamond ring glimmered like a thousand stars in the sky*. Do not overdo it and do not abuse your reader's trust. This is especially important when you are writing nonfiction prose, journalistic pieces, or academic assignments. Hyperbole has no place in factual writing and reporting. *See also* FIGURATIVE LANGUAGE.

RITE AID #7120

REGISTER 18 TRAN 08 07

CASHIER 02214

1 MERCHANDISE TAXABLE   .99 T
1 MERCHANDISE TAXABLE   .99 T
1 MERCHANDISE TAXABLE   .95 T
5 CETAPHIL CLEANSER 16OZ
                    10.79   53.95 T

8 ITEMS   SUB-TOTAL   62.88
                      TAX   3.15
                    TOTAL   66.03

    PAID BY MASTER   66.03
MASTER CARD # XXXXXXXXXXXX7115
EXP 2/28/99 APP # AUTO
REF # 277783
CARD PRESENT

          CASH CHANGE   .00

REFILL YOUR PRESCRIPTION ON THE
INTERNET AT WWW.RITEAID.COM
FOR YOUR LIFE. RITE AID'S GOT IT

Hyperurbanism

A faulty usage that results from overcompensating for common grammatical mistakes. People who use the famously incorrect phrase *between you and I* are usually overcompensating for the careless mistake of putting *me* in the subjective case: *You and me are friends*. The correct version of the latter sentence, *You and I are friends*, becomes so ingrained in one's mind that the phrase *you and me* never sounds correct. In fact, the phrase *between you and me* is grammatically correct. *See also* BETWEEN YOU AND I/MYSELF.

Hyphen

Hyphens are used to break up a word at the right margin of a page. The only correct place to hyphenate a word is at a syllable break: *pa-per; fil-ter*. Hyphens also join two-word adjectives; *cross-country; day-long*. Finally, hyphens are used in the spellings of numbers and fractions; *twenty-one; two-thirds*. Do not confuse hyphens with dashes. *See also* DASHES.

I

Idiom

Idioms are speech patterns that don't follow the standard rules of English. Many idioms include odd uses of prepositions, such as *put up with* or *hold up one's end of the deal*. Idioms are not incorrect, but they are generally informal. Some additional idioms: *abide by; capable of; impatient for; to part with; differ from; differ with; wait on somebody*.

i.e.

See E.G. VS. I.E.

Imperative mood

See MOOD: INDICATIVE, IMPERATIVE, SUBJUNCTIVE.

importantly

An adverb that is often used incorrectly in the phrases *more importantly* and *most importantly*. Use *more important* or *most important*.

in behalf

See BEHALF.

Inclusive language

Language that avoids use of male pronouns *he, him,* and *his* to refer to both men and women. Many older professional terms reflect a gender bias that assumes that women perform certain tasks and men perform others. In our society, obviously, this is not the case; language and pronouns now must reflect ambivalent gender roles to include both male and female capabilities. *Stewardess* has been replaced by *flight attendant*; *salesman* by *salesperson*; *anchorman* by *newscaster*. *Waitresses* and *actresses* can be referred to as *waiters* and *actors*; the gender delineations have been dropped. The constructions *his/her* and *him or her* have evolved as pronouns to the antecedent *one*, *anyone*, *a person*, and so on. For example: *Everyone needs to find his or her own niche.* Although this is awkward, it acknowledges that *everyone* could refer to either a male or a female. Use inclusive language in your writing and speaking to avoid insulting people and to avoid being perceived as sexist. *See also* GENDER; POLITICAL CORRECTNESS; *and* SEXIST LANGUAGE.

Incomplete comparison

A sentence that intends to compare two things but ultimately does not accomplish the task. Most incomplete comparisons are the result of comparative words like *such, so,* and *better.* If you write *This soup is much better*, you are making an incomplete comparison. You should write *This soup is much better than the chicken noodle.* Some more incomplete comparisons: *You are such a sweetheart; I'd rather go parasailing; Aspirin is better; Writing is more work.* Carry out the comparisons fully: *You are such a sweetheart that I adore you; I'd rather go parasailing than hang-gliding; Aspirin is better than ibuprofen; Writing is more work than reading.* Incomplete comparisons are extremely informal. Avoid them in your writing to ensure accuracy and clarity.

Indefinite pronoun

These are pronouns that do not indicate a specific person or a definite number of people or things: *anyone, anybody, no one, nobody, someone, somebody, each, none, most, another, both, few.* Most indefinite pronouns take singular verbs: *None is coming here; Each of us likes different colors.* Some indefinite pronouns take plural verbs: *Most are happy; Few of the participants attended.* Occasionally, some indefinite pronouns take both plural and singular verbs: *Some of the birds fly away; Some of the pie remains.*

Indented paragraph

See HUNG PARAGRAPH.

Independent clause

A clause that can stand alone as a complete sentence (containing a subject and verb). The underlined parts of the following examples are independent clauses: *If Jake chooses to go, <u>he will have to find his own ride</u>; <u>One of the trees has been struck by lightning</u>, but the rest of the forest seems fine.* Independent clauses can either stand alone or be combined with other independent and dependent clauses to form complex sentences. Remember, varying the types and lengths of your sentences is essential to good writing style.

Indian

See NATIVE AMERICAN; RACIAL, ETHNIC, AND RELIGIOUS TERMS.

Indirect quotation

See QUOTATION.

Infinitive

The basic form of a verb preceded by *to*: *to let; to go; to bungee jump; to lecture*. Infinitives can be used as nouns *(to bake is my favorite pastime)*, adverbs *(he went to the park to feed the birds)*, and adjectives *(you must resist the urge to yell)*. *See also* SPLIT INFINITIVE; VERB.

inflated diction

The use of exaggerated, hyperbolic, or long-winded language. When choosing your words, use descriptive and accurate terms, but don't overdo it. Don't use big words just for the sake of impressing your audience; you will alienate your readers and obscure the meaning you are attempting to communicate. This is inflated diction: *I have been engaged in the process of obfuscating the explicit denotation of my discourse, in particular by employing language that tends to be recondite, overwhelming, and multifarious*. This is the same idea expressed in clearer language: *I have complicated my ideas by using inappropriately complex language*. *See also* ABSTRACT DICTION *and* CLARITY.

Inflection

Changing the form of a word to indicate different meanings or grammatical uses. When verbs are inflected, it is called *conjugating* (*I am, you are, it is,* etc.); when nouns and pronouns are inflected, it is called *declension (woman, women, women's);* when adjectives and adverbs are inflected, it is called *comparison (good, better, best)*. Inflection incorporates passive and active voices, singular and plural nouns and pronouns, the various moods and voices, and so on. It is a mechanism built into the language to assure clarity, accuracy, and the adaptability of words to meanings.

Informal language

See FORMAL VS. INFORMAL LANGUAGE.

Initials

When writing to or about somebody whose name includes initials, insert a period and a space after the letter of the initial: *J. Edgar Hoover; E. M. Forster.* When referring to a completely initialized name, omit the periods and spaces: *LBJ; JFK.*

Intensive pronoun

A pronoun that amplifies the noun to which it refers: *I my-self will take out the trash; the thief herself brought back the stolen merchandise.* Use intensive pronouns to stress certain nouns without using italics or underlining: *I myself have not gone to the show, but I have heard wonderful things about it.* See also REFLEXIVE PRONOUN.

Interjection

A word such as *wow, gee, hey, ouch,* and *my goodness* that indicates an emotion of surprise, annoyance, wonder, or consent. Interjections are informal expressions and do not affect the grammatical structure of a sentence, although they should be set off with commas: *Wow, that is a hot plate! I would have helped, but hey, nobody called me.* The words *yes* and *no* can also be interjections: *No, there are not any size eights left.*

Interrogative pronoun

A pronoun that asks a question: *who, what, when, where, why, which, how.* See also INTERROGATIVE SENTENCE.

Interrogative sentence

A sentence that asks a question: *Where is the gas station?* Interrogative sentences usually end in a question mark *(Are you kidding?)* but can also end in an exclamation point *(Aren't you nice!)* or even a period *(Could you please return my sweater.).* Note the difference in tone that results from altering the punctuation of an interrogative sentence.

Irony

A conscious effort to say one thing and mean another. Irony can be humorous, caustic, or sarcastic. It is ironic to say *I've never felt better* directly after breaking your leg, or to say *Thanks for your concern* when someone is clearly not interested in your well-being. Irony is useful as a way to make a point or identify strange situations: *The expectant mother cared about many things: parties, cigarettes, late nights, good times. Strangely enough, she didn't seem to care about her unborn child as much as she cared about the finer things in life.* In this example, *the finer things* is being used ironically and sarcastically. The word *ironically* can be a very useful transition: *A plane carrying tons of illegal cargo crashed into the Pacific Ocean. Ironically, the rescue crews salvaged almost a ton of cocaine, but not one of the fifty passengers was saved.*

Italics

Used for emphasis and to set off titles of books *(East of Eden)*, plays *(Othello)*, movies *(The Wizard of Oz)*, television shows *(ER)*, long musical works *(The Nutcracker Suite)*, and published speeches *(The State of the Union)*. Italics are also used to identify foreign words and phrases *(voilà; ex post facto)* and names of ships *(The QE II)* and trains *(Metroliner)*. Wherever underlining is called for, use italics. The two are interchangeable, although in standard American English italics are preferred and underlining in considered outdated.

its vs. *it's*

Its is the possessive of *it,* and *it's* is a contraction meaning *it is: Its fur is soft and fluffy; It's only twenty degrees outside.* The confusion arises because of the *'s* phenomenon: people rightfully associate *'s* with possessives. However, in the case of *it,* the correct possessive is *its.*

J

Jargon

Specialized professional language. Most jargon seems complicated and incomprehensible to people who are not familiar with the topic. For instance, a person who is not familiar with computer terminology, might not know what these phrases mean: *crash the server; click the mouse; reformat the document; save on the c: drive.* A person who is not a lawyer might not understand these legal terms: *adversary proceeding; accord and satisfaction; metes and bounds; motion to dismiss.* Almost all disciplines, from academics (*discourse, paradigm*) to vehicle maintenance (*carburetor, transmission*) have developed a certain degree of jargon. Still, try to avoid using it in your writing. State things directly and precisely without resorting to technical babble. If you are certain that your readers will understand a nominal amount of jargon, you may use it if necessary. However, you might alienate your readers if you don't anticipate what they can or can't understand. Rewrite jargon-laden material until all cryptic terms have been explained or replaced.

Joke

See PUN.

Journalism

See MAGAZINE ARTICLE; NEWSPAPER ARTICLE.

Jr. and Sr.

Abbreviations for *Junior* and *Senior,* respectively. Usually preceded by a comma (although this is becoming optional), *Jr.* and *Sr.* always end with a period, even in the middle of a sentence or in combination with other punctuation; *Martin Luther King, Jr.'s speech made world history.*

Key words

The most important words in a sentence or paragraph. By virtue of being centrally important, key words tend to be repeated several times. You can use variations of the key words to keep your writing lively and prevent redundancy. For example, if the key word of an essay is *change,* you can alternately use *modification, transformation, growth, shift, variation, fluctuation, metamorphosis,* or *deviation* to prevent the word *change* from becoming trite. A good thesaurus is very helpful here.

kind of

A slang qualifier that means *somewhat* or *slightly.* Avoid *kind of* in all writing. Use a more appropriate expression: *moderately; partially; quite; rather. This casserole is kind of too salty* should be written *This casserole is overly salty.*

lady

An antiquated term for *woman.* Some people perceive *lady* as sexist; avoid using the word in your writing. *See also* GENDER; SEXIST LANGUAGE.

lain vs. laid

See LAY VS. LIE.

Language level

The level of readability based on vocabulary, sentence structure, and tone. This correlates directly to knowing and understanding your audience's expectations. Don't write at a high reading level for an elementary school pamphlet; similarly, don't treat an audience of academicians as if they were totally ignorant. Use complex vocabulary only if it suits your meaning, not as a way to impress your readers. *See also* AUDIENCE; INFLATED DICTION.

Latina

A female descendant of the people of any of the various Latin American countries. *See also* RACIAL, ETHNIC, AND RELIGIOUS TERMS.

Latino

A male descendant of the people of any of the various Latin American countries. *See also* RACIAL, ETHNIC, AND RELIGIOUS TERMS.

latter

See FORMER VS. LATTER.

lay vs. lie

Although they seem as if they are related to one another, these two verbs are entirely separate in meaning and usage. *Lay* (which includes the forms *lay, laid,* and *laid*) means to put something in a specified place. It is a transitive verb, meaning that it always takes a direct object: *I lay the clothes on the bed. Lie* (which includes the forms *lie, lay,* and *lain*) means to rest horizontally on a surface. It is intransitive, meaning that it never takes a direct object: *I lie on the bed.*

lead vs. *led*

Lead is the present tense of the verb meaning to show or take charge: *I can lead you to the treasure*. *Led* is the past participle of this verb: *I have led you to believe that I am clever*.

led

See LEAD VS. LED.

Length

If you are writing for a specific purpose—a newspaper deadline, an essay, a term paper, an obituary—you must stick to the page- or word-length guidelines that have been assigned to you. A ten-page paper obviously needs to be about that long (not nineteen pages or eight pages), and must include the amount of research, insight, and original thought necessary to sustain ten pages of good writing and solid ideas. If you submit a paper that is several pages short on length or cheats in terms of overly large margins and spacing on the tops and bottom of pages, you are in danger of failing because you have not followed instructions. (Every page should be double-spaced, contain one-inch margins on all sides, and consist of roughly 225 words.) Similarly, if you write too much, your teacher will still have reason to give you a poor grade. If you find that you are significantly over or under your requirement after you have completed your first draft, make it a priority to cut or add text appropriately.

less

See FEWER VS. LESS.

let's

A contraction for the words *let us*. This informal phrase usually prefaces a suggestion: *Let's go to the party*. The implied subject of this imperative sentence is *you*: *You let us go to the party*. Avoid *let's* in formal writing. See also MOOD: INDICATIVE, IMPERATIVE, SUBJUNCTIVE.

Letter

See BUSINESS LETTER; COMPLAINT, LETTER OF; *and* PERSONAL LETTER.

Library research

Research is a detail-oriented labor that will generally require access to a school, university, or public library. Whether you need encyclopedias, medical journals, newspaper articles, census information, electronic databases, or other types of data, chances are your library will either have it on hand or be able to locate it for you. Research begins with identifying your topic: narrowing it down into a manageable size; zeroing in on a specific area of interest; defining the time period; defining the historical, geographical, and social context; planning out the extensiveness of your project; and so on. The next stage is gathering information: reading, taking notes, photocopying, and looking up related topics. Keep at it until you feel you have obtained enough material for your purpose or have exhausted the library's available information on your topic. Make an outline to organize the information you have been collecting. Some people use index cards or a designated notebook to keep their sources organized and accessible. Always keep detailed records of where you obtained a piece of information for documentation in your bibliography. The last step in research is writing; don't jump the gun by beginning this step before you are satisfied that you have enough raw material to work from. Otherwise, you will find yourself spending unnecessary time returning to the library and looking up the same things all over again.

lie

See LAY VS. LIE.

like

See AS VS. LIKE.

List

In prose writing, lists or series that run in with your text can be boring and monotonous. This sentence is tedious and poorly written: *I woke up this morning and did the following chores: made my bed, ate cereal for breakfast, cleaned the upstairs bathroom with bleach, put a load of laundry in the washer, made some phone calls, took the dog for a walk around the block, vacuumed, and washed the dishes.* If you must use lists, be sure to form parallel list elements by matching the structure of each element. Revision: *I woke up this morning and did several chores: made the bed, ate my breakfast, cleaned the bathroom, washed the clothes, made some phone calls, walked the dog, vacuumed the rugs, and did the dishes.* The verb forms are consistent, allowing for better flow. In business writing, it is acceptable to create bulleted lists, which are more formal and utilitarian than series sentences:

The meeting will address these concerns:
- *employee benefits*
- *the new union regulations*
- *security guidelines and precautions*
- *revised branch management policies*

Lists are usually introduced by colons, and elements therein are separated by commas or semicolons. Avoid using lists in prose that should be vivid and descriptive. *See also* PARALLEL STRUCTURE.

Literally

As opposed to *figuratively*, *literally* means "by the word." If you write *The man literally weighed five hundred pounds*, you mean that he could step on to a scale and weigh in at a quarter of a ton. If you write *The man weighs a ton*, you have created a figurative reference, meaning that the man is extremely overweight but does not truly weigh 2,000 pounds. The adverb *literally* is overused in casual dialogue (*I will literally die if he doesn't show up* is actually a figurative sentence) and should be used cautiously in formal writing. *See also* FIGURATIVE LANGUAGE.

little

The comparative forms of *little* when referring to quantity are irregular: *little, less, least. Little* when referring to size is regular: *little, littler, littlest.*

logic

See ARGUMENT; CONTINUITY; AND ORGANIZATION.

M

Magazine article

When writing for a magazine, start by asking the following questions: Who is my audience? What is the purpose of this article? What is the topic I will be writing about? How long must the article be? When is it due? How much time do I have to research and write it? Some of these questions, such as the length of the article and the due date, will probably will be answered by your editor. These parameters will be important in determining the scope and depth of an article.

When beginning an article, keep your audience in mind. The tone of an article for a science trade journal will probably be much drier than a piece on fashion for a women's magazine. If you are unfamiliar with the style of the publication to which you are submitting your article, acquaint yourself with it by reading a few back copies. You must have a clear idea of the tone and style of writing expected of you before you start writing. It is also a good idea to ask your editor for a house style sheet, so you can follow the Magazine's format and rules of presentation.

Flexibility should also play a significant role in the writing of a magazine article. Bear in mind that your article may be reshaped by your editor or truncated because of space constraints. The editor may ask you for rewrites and revision as well. Unless you have a well-supported reason for disagreeing with the editor's requests, fulfill them cheerfully and on schedule. *See also* AUDIENCE; FOCUS.

Malapropism

A humorous misapplication of a word; the use of a word sounding similar to the intended one but ridiculously wrong in the given context: *I represent (resent) that remark.*

Masculine

See GENDER; SEXIST LANGUAGE.

may vs. *can*

Be sure to distinguish clearly between *may*, which suggests permission or potential to act, and *can*, which refers to physical ability or opportunity to act: *Cathy may pass home plate, but only if she can hit the ball out of the field.*

m-dash

See DASH.

Memo

A form of communication, less formal than a letter, between members of an organization. A memo usually has the word *MEMO* or *MEMORANDUM* across the top, and usually contains the following information:

Date:
To:
From:
Subject: (or Re:)

The abbreviation *cc* (standing for "carbon copy") at the bottom of a memo precedes the names of other parties receiving the document.

When writing a memo, it is best to use formal language. Get your point across quickly and coherently. A memo's purpose is to convey an idea or instruction in a clear and direct manner. Memos are usually brief; if you find yourself going on for more than a page or two, you may want to consider rewriting it in another format.

Metaphor

A word or phrase that implies a comparison or identity. Metaphors can enrich your writing by adding unexpected dimensions to your words: *He was as thick as a whale omelet.* This device should be used carefully, however, as many comparisons have become clichéd from overuse: *The sun shone like gold. See* also SIMILE.

Minutes

The record of a meeting is called the minutes. Minutes are an impartial account of the business accomplished at a specific meeting. Well-recorded and well-constructed minutes make meetings more effective by reminding the participants and others of what was discussed and decided, and by highlighting the decisions that were made. They also allow participants to reflect on the meeting with a sense of perspective. Often, the first agenda item in a meeting is the review and approval of the previous meeting's minutes. This ensures that the minutes are an accurate representation of the meeting, and reminds the participants where they left off.

Minutes generally contain the following information: date, time and place of the meeting; the name of the company; the type of meeting; names of those attending; whether or not the minutes from the previous meeting were read and approved; and a summary of what happened at the meeting. The following is an example:

The Lutheran Layperson's League
67 Agnes Road
New York, NY 10056

May 3, 1996

As scheduled, The Lutheran Layperson's League had its weekly meeting at 7 P.M. on Friday, May 3, at the Education Building. In attendance were Pastor Wright, Chairman Bill Pulito, Secretary Sherry Mintz, and Treasurer Wanda Allbright. The minutes from last week's meeting were reviewed and approved by all in attendance.

The following topics were covered: the annual fundraising campaign; the mission budget; the quarterly convocation in Missouri, which all board members will attend; and the possibility of creating a turnaround driveway at the Lutheran Community Center. The last topic will be discussed further at next week's meeting, which is slated to begin at 7 P.M. Friday, May 10.

—Joel Serpentine, Clerk

Misplaced modifier

A common mistake in writing is misplaced adverbs or adjectives, which leave readers in doubt of your intended meaning. You can avoid misplacing modifiers by carefully editing your writing, noting all adjectives and adverbs (especially those that are lengthy or complex), and double-checking that they are clearly linked to the words they modify.

Pay special attention to inverted sentences, in which phrases or clauses are often not close to the words they modify. The following is an example of a sentence containing a misplaced modifier: *Swimming rapidly, the boy was saved by the lifeguard. Swimming rapidly* seems to modify *the boy* when it is intended to modify *the lifeguard*. A more correct sentence would be: *Swimming rapidly, the lifeguard saved the boy.*

Mixed metaphor

When a writer makes an inconsistent or faulty comparison between two things, she or he has created a mixed metaphor. Keeping in mind a clear picture of what you are attempting to express figuratively will help ensure consistent metaphors. The following example contains a mixed metaphor: *The novelist wielded sarcasm as a knife to illustrate his anger.* The words *wielded* and *knife* are poorly matched with the word *il-*

lustrate. The following sentence corrects the mixed metaphor: *The novelist used sarcasm as a tool to illustrate his anger.*

Mood: indicative, imperative, subjunctive

In addition to tense and voice, verbs have moods indicating feelings or attitudes toward the action they describe.

The indicative mood is used for all statements, questions, and so on that are not in the imperative or subjunctive moods. It is the neutral mood in which a writer expresses what is believed to be fact or evident, or reports what others have assumed to be correct: *Some mammals estivate in the summer, but most hibernate in the winter.*

The imperative mood is used for commands or requests: *Go to your room, but keep your stereo off.* Imperative statements are frequently marked by inversions or other unusual word order, and they often end in exclamation points to further distinguish their mood.

The subjunctive mood, also called the conditional mood, is used to express matters that are not always actual or accepted. Wishes and commands fall into this category. Example: *If I tell her, she may get upset and cancel the lunch date.* Subjunctive sentences are often preceded by the introductory words *if* or *that.*

You should not mix moods in your sentences. WRONG: *Tell him to move the dresser, and you should ask him for an invoice.* RIGHT: *Tell him to move the dresser, and ask him for an invoice.*

Multiculturalism

An awareness of and respect for different cultural, religious, and ethnic groups. With constantly improving forms of transportation and communication, and with the media and many businesses becoming international in scope, people all over the world are having to deal with others who do not share many of the same cultural values, preferences, customs, and language. This broadening of views has translated into a heightened

sensitivity to many cultures, and writers should be aware of
the probable diversity of their readers. A business proposition
read in Los Angeles or New York may also be read in Singa-
pore and Japan. Your coworkers may have been born in Mexico or Cuba. People want to see that your thoughts are
relevant to them. When writing for a culturally diverse audience, pay particular attention to your word choices. Use formal language and avoid idioms and colloquialisms that might
not be clearly understood. If the situation warrants it, research
the culture of the people you are trying communicate with to
ensure that you are conveying your thoughts in a cogent manner. *See also* GENDER; RACIAL, ETHNIC AND RELIGIOUS TERMS.

myself
See REFLEXIVE PRONOUN.

N

Name
See CAPITALIZATION; FORM OF ADDRESS.

Narrative
The function of narrative writing is to tell a story. Narrative
writing recounts events in succession. Following is an example of narrative writing.

*After the wedding ceremony, Melanie and John stayed behind
because they wanted to reflect on their vows with no one
around. They climbed to the tower on the top of the church and
looked out over the town. For a long time, they simply em-
braced and said nothing.*

*Shortly thereafter, the Rolls-Royce they had rented for the oc-
casion arrived, and they were escorted to the reception hall.
John's Aunt Eunice, who had fallen ill recently and had not*

been able to attend the ceremony, made a surprise appearance.
Everyone danced until dawn, and Melanie and John left the fol-
lowing morning for their honeymoon.

Native American

A preferred term for pre-1492 inhabitants of the Americas.
The term *Indian* is somewhat problematic: it is inaccurate,
based on a mistaken European conception of geography; also,
it is a name that was given to a people, not chosen by them.
In addition, the term has some negative connotations, such as
in *Indian giver.*

When the specific cultural group or tribe you are referring
to is known, such as *Sioux, Apache,* or *Cheyenne,* use that
name in favor of the term *Native American.* See also RACIAL,
ETHNIC, AND RELIGIOUS TERMS.

Negative form

See POSITIVE FORM.

Negro

See RACIAL, ETHNIC, AND RELIGIOUS TERMS.

neither . . . nor

See CORRELATIVE CONJUNCTIONS.

Netiquette

Also known as *internet etiquette,* this term refers to the social conventions and standards of politeness commonly used
on the Internet. It is a good idea to observe the following
guidelines when sending and receiving electronic mail:

Assume that everyone has access to your e-mail communi-
cations. It is easy to send and resend files; for example, rela-
tively new users of the Internet may experiment with batch
sending and accidentally post a private note of yours to several people for whom it was not intended. The same rule applies to business correspondence; an innocent jab at your boss
sent to a coworker might accidentally wind up in your boss'

lap, subject to interpretation. If you are not comfortable with the fact that your privacy on the Internet is not always guaranteed, it is better not to send mail that could yield undesirable consequences.

Realize the limitations of the medium. Unlike an in-person meeting or even a telephone conversation, e-mail correspondence can not carry the subtle messages conveyed by facial expressions and vocal inflections. Make sure your words represent precisely what you want to say, and avoid ambiguity of tone—what you intend as sarcasm might not come across that way on the Internet.

Understand that your mail might not be read at the time you are sending it. Your message may not reach the intended person until hours or even days after you've sent it. Particularly in areas of business correspondence, always clearly express what you are writing about, as some people receive dozens, even hundreds, of e-mail messages a day and anything that doesn't appear important may get tossed.

Do not use exclamation points or all capital letters. E-mail messages laden with exclamation points and capital letters are hard to read, are visually annoying, and actually de-emphasize the important points of the correspondence.

Be brief. People do not like to read long letters on a computer screen. Be quick and to the point.

Proofread. Do not take e-mail lightly. A spelling mistake in business correspondence sent via e-mail will reflect on you the same way as in a general letter and may prove costly.

Cite sources. If you are sending material from another source—printed or from the Internet—identify the author and publisher as you would in a normal bibliography. Information garnered on the Internet is not necessarily public domain, which could make you liable for plagiarism if you aren't careful. If the source is public domain, you still need to identify it, so readers can refer to it for further information.

On a final note, adhere to the rules of grammar and writing style expressed in this book to ensure that your e-mail messages are concise, coherent, and stylistically sound.

Neuter

See GENDER.

Newspaper article

A newspaper article should answer the questions *who, what, when, where,* and *why,* preferably in the first sentence or two. The rest of the article is commentary, detail, implications for the future, and context for the event. Use active words whenever possible, and plenty of verbs. Newspaper article writing is traditionally sparse, leaving deeper narrative writing for magazines. The first paragraph of a newspaper article is called the lead. Its purpose is to immediately grab the reader's attention. Decide which of the interrogative words is most appropriate for the piece your writing. In an article about the return of the Luciano Pavarotti vocal competition to Philadelphia, the *what* is most important, and should go first:

> *The Luciano Pavarotti Vocal Competition returned to Philadelphia last night after a three-year hiatus, and featured a visit from the beaming tenor himself. The competition had been held in New York the last three years, which many critics viewed as an insult to the opera community at large.*

In a straight news story, the least important facts go at the end because editors often need to shorten articles to make room for late-breaking news. Every paragraph of your news story should be an acceptable place to end a complete account. Even the first paragraph of the Pavarotti story is adequate: It answers four of the five questions, and raises the reader's interest about the *why.*

When writing a newspaper article, you should heed a few guidelines. The most important quality of all journalism is accuracy. Make sure your facts are straight and double-check all quotations. Journalistic integrity also requires objectivity, or the ability not to favor one side over the other. All reporters know that this is close to impossible, but strive to achieve it nonetheless.

non sequitur

Latin term meaning "it does not follow." In standard usage, a non sequitur is used to describe a statement or idea that follows another chronologically but not logically: *We're going to Utah in August; I'm taking the laundry across the street.*

not only . . . but also

See CORRELATIVE CONJUNCTIONS.

Noun

Words that name people, places, things, or ideas, in the broadest sense, are called nouns: *dog; tree;* and *mug.* Nouns function in a variety of ways in sentences—as subjects, objects, and other parts of speech. Nouns have number: They can be singular when referring to one thing or person, and plural when naming more than one. In the plural, most nouns change form, adding *s.* Nouns also have gender when they refer to people. Finally, nouns have case, which refers to the role they play in a sentence: nominative case for subjects or subject complements (predicate nouns); objective case for objects of verbs; and possessive case for ownership forms, usually marked with an apostrophe and an *s,* or just an apostrophe.

Nouns that are used as names of individual things or people are called proper nouns, and are usually capitalized to indicate that function: *Titanic, Pope John Paul II, Cheryl.*

Nouns must agree with their verbs—a singular noun takes a singular verb, a plural noun takes a plural verb, and so on. The gerund (*-ing* form) of a verb can function as a noun: *Listening is a skill. See also* AGREEMENT.

Noun clause

When nouns, verbs, and other words are combined into clauses, they can play any role in a sentence that a noun can play: *What you are looking for is right under your nose.* The noun clause *What you are looking for* is the subject in this sentence, though it could be the object of an active verb (*I know what you are looking for*), or the object of a preposition

(Let's talk about what you are looking for), or a predicate noun *(This is what you are looking for)*.

Noun clauses usually begin with relative pronouns such as *that, what, whatever, which, whichever, who, whoever, whom, whomever,* or *whose.*

number vs. amount

See AMOUNT VS. NUMBER.

Numbers

Numbers follow two different styles: they can be spelled out *(twenty-five)* or written in figures *(25)*. There are cardinal numbers (noun forms, such as *twenty-five*), and ordinal numbers (adjectival forms such as *twenty-fifth* or *25th*).

Ordinals suggest ranking, while cardinals denote quantity: *Twenty-five is the twenty-fifth number.* Ordinals are commonly formed by adding *-th: Consolation prizes were awarded to the fourth-, fifth- and sixth-place winners.* Note that some numbers have their own ordinal forms: *Trophies will be given to first-, second- and third-place winners.* Compound numbers change only their last element into an ordinal form: *five hundredth; five hundred and first.* Cardinals are like all other nouns, and, with the exception of *zero* and *one,* they are all plural. Numbers treated as words in and of themselves, however, can be singular or plural: *He placed a one at the top of the chart and two sevens at the bottom.* In this example, the numbers represent written forms; consequently, they can be said to have number.

In standard American usage, numbers under 100 are usually written out. This is especially true of ordinal numbers, which are commonly spelled out no matter what their length. In some business and scientific writing, however, it is acceptable to use figures to represent cardinal numbers. Ordinals vary, but generally there is more tolerance for usage for terms like *204th* in scientific, economic, and other technical styles. Newspaper writing and other forms of writing where space is limited may favor figures because they are shorter and more visible. Whatever style you choose, it is important to remain consistent throughout the entire piece you are writing.

Note that spelled-out cardinal numbers include hyphens for all numbers over twenty and below one hundred that are compound forms containing two or more numbers: *three hundred and sixty-five days in a year.* Longer ordinal compounds are also hyphenated when used as adjectives with nouns present: *I see the fifty-first hash mark.*

When beginning a sentence with a number, you should spell it out: *Two hundred and forty-three people came to our wedding.* In some cases, however, figures are required:

- addresses, as in *235 Sullivan Street*
- years, as in *1986*
- phone numbers, as in *(212) 675-9876*
- large and/or exact amounts, as in *7.6 million dollars*
- decimals and fractions, as in *8.25% tax; 33/4*
- sports scores, as in *Mets win 3–1*

In these cases, if the number falls at the beginning of the sentence, rewrite to place the numeral later in the sentence.

Objectivity
See EXPOSITORY WRITING; OPINION

obligated vs. *obliged*

Obligated refers to a sense of duty: *I am obligated to teach until 1997.* The word *obliged* has two different meanings: "forced" or "constrained" *(I was obliged to pay my library fines before I was allowed to take out any new books)* or "grateful" *(I'd be much obliged to you if you would throw me that life preserver).*

of vs. *'ve*

A similarity in spoken language has led to this grammatical confusion in writing. WRONG: *You could of warned me about their dirty tricks.* RIGHT: *You could've warned me about their dirty tricks.* The proper form is *could've,* a contraction of *could have,* not *could of.* Also watch out for *should have/should've* and *would have/would've.* Neither of these phrases uses the word *of.* If you are not sure which is correct, *'ve* or *of,* say the sentence out loud with *have* replacing *'ve* or *of:* WRONG: *I'd like a cup have tea.* RIGHT: *I'd like a cup of tea.*

on vs. *upon*

Use *upon* to convey the sense of *on top of,* as in: *She placed the ring upon the pillow.* Generally, *on* can be used in place of *upon* in other situations. You will hear when the two words have different meanings in a given sentence: *The little girl jumped on the bed* could mean she jumped on it once and stayed there for some time, or that she bounced up and down repeatedly. Some idiomatic phrases distinguish between the two: *upon my word; put upon; imposed on.*

on behalf

See BEHALF.

opinion

When writing an objective piece, be careful not to let your own opinions taint the impartiality of your words. Whenever you write, you are in danger of slipping in your own views disguised as fact without noticing it. Pay special attention to introductory phrases such as *the fact is, the fact of the matter,* and *in actual fact*—often, they indicate a place in your writing where an opinion may be masquerading as a fact.

Oral presentation

Oral presentations are different from writing in one important respect: structure. The reason for the directness of oral presentations is for the speaker to prepare the audience for what they are going to hear. If you are presenting a list, introduce the list with a general category, or with a question that will allow the audience to process the list in the way you want:

> *Here are some of the most important peace activists of this century: Gandhi, Ham Sok Hon, Hammarskjold. . . .*
> *What do the following women have in common? Shere Hite, Germaine Greer, Aletta Jacobs, and Dora Russell.*

The most important part of the writing of an oral presentation is a tight structure. Your language can be formal or conversational; your cadence can be in the form of a strong argument or a verbal instruction; but bear in mind that if you ramble, your audience's attention may stray. Make sure you deliver your message clearly, and be sure to provide enough information to support your ideas. It is also important to know when you've sufficiently made your point. Knowing when to stop is an indispensable skill. At the end of your oral presentation, recapitulate the main points of your speech, and finish with a clear and definite conclusion.

Order
See ORGANIZATION.

ORGANIZATION

A common failing among novice writers is that they present everything in a jumble of topics and messages. When the message is long and complex, it is harder to maintain order and even more crucial that a system of organization be imposed on its elements.

In general, the organization will be dictated by the kind of writing. A newspaper article answers basic factual questions. A magazine article grabs the reader's attention. A report or research paper describes the question that the piece will address and explains its importance.

The organization of a work of nonfiction often is determined by some principle of logic. There are two basic orientations that determine the relationship between theory and data: deductive reasoning and inductive reasoning. Deductive reasoning begins with theories, and seeks facts to support those theories. A deductive argument might be:

There is a history of poor management that clearly demonstrates why we did not win zoning approval. In March, we canceled the county's ten-mile "Race for the Cure." In May, we ignored the petition concerning corporate garbage dumping in the North River. And in December, there were three fatal accidents at the intersection of Main Street and Route 11, following repeated attempts by the citizens of this county to have a four-way traffic light installed at the intersection.

The other orientation, inductive reasoning, begins with facts and generalizes theories from them. When you use this technique, you allow your audience to draw their own conclusions along with you, rather than being compelled to accept or reject yours:

In March, we canceled the county's ten-mile "Race for the Cure." In May, we ignored the petition concerning corporate garbage dumping in the North River. And in December, there were three fatal accidents at the intersection of Main Street and Route 11, following repeated attempts by the citizens of this county to have a four-way traffic light installed at the intersection. Could it be that our failure to win zoning approval is linked to this history of events?

The conclusion is often the most difficult part of a piece. A rule of thumb is to connect the ending with the beginning. If your opening sentence contains metaphorical language, so should your conclusion. The circular structure will alert your reader that your piece is ending, and will give it a sense of closure.

Oriental

An out-of-date term for someone or something originating from China, Japan, Vietnam, Korea, or other countries of East Asia. *Asian* is preferred; however, when possible, it is best to

refer to the specific country of origin. *See also* RACIAL, ETH-
NIC, AND RELIGIOUS TERMS.

Outline

A means of organizing thoughts in preparation for writing,
and a way of presenting the main ideas without the details.
Outlines are useful for almost any classification of writing.
They provide writers with a road map that prevents them from
wandering too far off a topic.

Don't be afraid that if you create an outline before beginning to write, you will lock yourself into something that cannot be altered. The outline is a flexible tool. You can deviate
from it; its great advantage is that you will recognize when
you are deviating.

The basic outline begins with major headings, which can
correspond to chapters of a book, paragraphs of an essay, sections of a report, etc. The major headings are denoted with uppercase roman numerals; the next level down by uppercase
letters; the next level, arabic numerals; then lowercase letters;
and finally, lowercase roman numerals:

The Art of Therapeutic Massage

  I. Introduction

 II. History of Massage
    A. China
    B. India
    C. Sweden

III. Modern Techniques
    A. Swedish
      1. Strokes
        a. Petrissage
        b. Effleurage
        c. Tapotement
      2. Full Body Treatment

IV. Benefits of Massage
    A. Relaxation

B. Reduced Stress
C. Increased Flexibility

V. Conclusion

Overstatement
See HYPERBOLE.

Paragraphing
The basic building block of prose writing. In expository writing, each paragraph begins with a topic sentence, and then expands on the idea contained therein, or offers support for it. Each paragraph should be able to stand alone as a meaningful or clear statement. If you are unsure, take the paragraph out of context, give it to a reader, and see if he or she can derive meaning from it.

Parallel structure
Parallel constructions are phrases or clauses within the same sentence that repeat the same word forms (nouns, verbs, adjectives, and so on) in the same order to provide clarity. Unlike agreement, parallelism is not grammatically essential. However, it can lend a sense of unity to your writing and help you convey your thoughts and ideas more effectively:

> *We decided to go to the museum instead of the park because it looked like it was going to rain, the kids wanted to see the dinosaurs, and the museum was within walking distance.*

Each subordinate clause (*It looked like it was going to rain/the kids wanted to see the dinosaurs/the museum was within walking distance*) in this sentence follows the pattern *noun, verb, predicate.* This repetition adds harmony and consistency to the writing. However, parallelism does not mean that every single sentence should follow the exact same patterns. Variety of structure within the general guidelines of parallelism can give your readers a sense of the relative weights and moods of objects, thoughts, or ideas in your writing.

Using lists or numbers to introduce paragraphs and separate ideas calls attention to parallelism. The things listed or numbered should be more or less equal in weight or importance: *He went to the bank, the grocer, the dry cleaner, and the place where he grew up, where he visited with his mother and old friends for a long time.* It is better to write: *He went to the bank, the grocer, and the dry cleaner. After these errands, he went to the place where he grew up,. . . .*

One of the most frequent infractions of parallel structure is using it with incongruous lengths or weights of elements. For instance, the combination of a short clause with a longer one violates the rules of parallelism and can be jarring to your reader. Unless you prepare your reader for an upcoming imbalance or are striving for profound effect by using abruptly imbalanced lengths, your writing will probably profit from having elements of approximately the same length perform approximately the same function. *See also* CADENCE.

Paraphrasing

Restating, explaining, and/or augmenting the ideas and thoughts contained in another source, such as a text, passage, or other written work. When paraphrasing, pay close attention to how much of the original source you have retained; if you are relating another's words close to verbatim, you will need to acknowledge the source. *See also* CITATION; QUOTATION.

Parentheses

A set of punctuation marks frequently used to set off interjections or supplemental materials: *The flowers (roses, carnations, and sweetpeas) will be shipped to your home.*

Parenthetical expressions use different forms of punctuation, depending partially on the degree of independence of the thought they enclose. If an entire sentence appears within the parentheses, so should its end punctuation: *(However, it appears that lately this is not the case.)*

When parentheses enclose phrases or clauses, all punctuation required by the sentence outside the parentheses is placed outside: *The office manager, Ellis Cooper (who has been working with us for five years), will show you how to use the computer system.* In this example, a comma follows the last parenthesis because it is needed to set off the following phrase. If the sentence had required a semicolon, colon, or period, these marks would also have fallen outside the last parenthesis.

Parenthetical expressions may require internal punctuation in order to make them understandable: *The temperature dipped below freezing (again!), and the windchill factor made it dangerous to be outside.* See also BRACKETS.

Parenthetical documentation

See CITATION.

Passive voice

See VOICE: ACTIVE, PASSIVE.

Past tense

See TENSE: PAST, PRESENT, FUTURE.

Person

See POINT OF VIEW.

Personal letter

When writing a personal letter, you can break grammatical rules as long as you communicate your message in a style your reader will understand. Unlike a business letter, the salutation on a personal letter is often followed by a comma, not a colon. *Dear Judy* is preferable to *To Whom It May Concern.* Generally, one ends with a sentiment that is warmer than one would use in a business letter: *Love, Truman; With fondest wishes for a happy married life together, Jack; Yours in ever-lasting gratitude, Martha.*

The following is an example of a personal letter:

John Whittier
29 Bakersfield Road
Elmsville, Illinois

November 23, 1996

Dear Lisa,

I just wanted to thank you for having me over for dinner the other night. I had a wonderful time, and I hope you'll let me return the favor soon. Your new home is beautiful; you really have a flair for decorating. Talk to you on Friday, and thanks again!

Love,

John

Personal pronouns

Personal pronouns indicate specific persons or things: *I, you, he, she, it, we,* and *they.* The first-person pronoun is *I,* while the plural form is *we.* The second-person pronoun is *you;* the plural form is also *you.* There are three third-person pronouns: *she, he,* and *it.* The plural form for all three is *they.*

Personal pronouns refer to either *the person speaking, the person spoken to,* or *the person or thing spoken of.* The following sentences show the usage of personal pronouns in the first, second, and third person:

I am going to the post office. (*I* is the person speaking.)
You are going to the thrift shop. (*You* is the person spoken to.)
She was late for the meeting. (*She* is the person spoken about.)
We are trying to repair the oil leak. (*We* refers to the persons speaking.)
They have a summer house. (*They* refers to the persons spoken about.)
It was a cold, rainy night. (*It* refers to the thing spoken about.)

Personal pronouns also have different forms to indicate case, which are shown in the following list:

Forms of the personal pronouns:

First person:
Pronouns referring to the speaker:
  I, me, mine (singular)
  we, ours, our (plural)

Second person:
Pronouns referring to the person spoken to:
  you, yours, your (singular & plural)

Third person:
Pronouns referring to the person(s) or thing(s) spoken about:
  she, her, he, his, it, its (singular)
  they, their, theirs, them (plural)

Place names

Proper names of places are capitalized: *Seattle; Washington*. When they are part of a proper name, common nouns and adjectives are capitalized as well: *Bluestone Lake; South America*. However, descriptive words referring to places with inexact boundaries are set in lowercase: *the southern part of the region*.

Also, note that some local terms are commonly capitalized: *Greenwich Village* (New York); *Bay Area* (San Francisco).

Plagiarism

When you quote an author or paraphrase an idea other than your own without citing the source, you are plagiarizing. When writing, make sure to meticulously cite your sources. Careless mistakes could possibly infringe upon someone else's copyright. *See also* BIBLIOGRAPHY; CITATION

Poetry

When citing poetry, try to retain as much of the original spacing and line breaks as possible. Example:

To me, fair friend, you can never be old,
For as you were when I first your eye I ey'd,

> *Such seems your beauty still.*
>   *—William Shakespeare*

When lines of poetry are run in, use slashes to indicate line breaks, and be sure to retain the original punctuation and capitalization. When text is omitted, be sure to insert ellipses (three dots).

> *For where thou art or shalt be, there or here;/And this . . . this lute and song . . . loved yesterday,/(The singing angels know) are only dear/Because thy name moves right in what they say.*
>   *—Elizabeth Barrett Browning*

Point of view

There are three ways in which a writer can communicate: first person, second person, and third person. First person uses the pronoun *I,* meaning that unless the work is a piece of fiction told through a character, the writer is the voice of the piece. Second person uses the pronoun *you,* indicating that the writer intends to address the reader directly. Third person, the standard in nonfiction, is told without either pronoun and represents an objective, distanced voice. While all three points of view are acceptable depending on the type of narrative and on the specific work itself, it is unacceptable to switch point of view within a sentence or paragraph; generally speaking, it is best to keep the point of view consistent through the entire work as well, to avoid confusion.

Political correctness

The attempt to rid the English language of sexist, racist, and all other discriminatory language. All writers should be sensitive to potentially offensive wording in their work. For instance, generically using the word *he* or *him* subsumes women's identities into men's and represents outdated social implications: *The doctor went in to see the patient, then he made a diagnosis.* This sentence reads as sexist, since not all doctors are men.

When writing about race and ethnicity, be careful not to marginalize groups or make it seem that they deviate from the cultural norm. Also, try not to impose definitions on people;

if you are not sure what to call a group, ask members of the group itself. For instance, the phrase *physically challenged* is now the preferred term for an individual who uses a wheelchair; however, some peope may find this patronizing and still prefer the original word, disabled.

Bear in mind that while you are writing and striving to be sensitive to the rights of others, you can sometimes go overboard. An example might be calling a dwarf *vertically challenged.* Terms that are overly euphemistic can be unintentionally funny or demeaning. However, understand that the main ideology behind political correctness is to counter the stigmas, prejudices, and stereotypes often created by insensitive language. *See also* RACIAL, ETHNIC, AND RELIGIOUS TERMS; SEXIST LANGUAGE.

Positive form

Instead of *He really didn't have a flair for home economics,* use a positive statement such as *He was a bad cook.* We often hedge our statements, use bland and unassertive language, and minimize our observations. To make sure that your readers clearly understand your message, say exactly what you mean.

Possessive

See APOSTROPHE.

Possessive case

See CASE; SUBJECTIVE, OBJECTIVE, POSSESSIVE.

Possessive pronoun

Pronouns form possessives in distinctive ways. Indefinite pronouns follow the rules listed below, adding *'s* in most cases. Personal pronouns have unique possessive forms. Most singular nouns add an apostrophe and an *s* to form a possessive: *The dog's tail is wagging.* In the plural, nouns that end in *s* add only an apostrophe: *The dogs' tails are wagging.* Collective nouns that do not end in *s* add both the apostrophe and the *s: The au-*

dience's reaction was positive. Singular nouns or names that end in *s* add an apostrophe and an *s* to form the possessive: *James's report was compared favorably to Bess's.* Some styles form possessives for important names that end in *s* with just an apostrophe *(Moses', Jesus')*. Unless you are required to follow such a style, add *'s.*

When more than two things or people possess something, you need to determine whether the ownership is combined or joint or whether each one has an equal and separate share. In the first case, show joint ownership by two or more people or things by making only the last word possessive: *Carl and Tabitha's new play is captivating.* In the second case, show individual ownership by making each person or thing possessive: *Ripken's and Mattingly's playing were spectacular.*

If you are unsure as to whether each person's contribution to or ownership of something is shared or distinct, it is probably better to assume separate possessives than to run the risk of offending someone by slighting her or his role. This is particularly true for married couples and parent-child teams. It is considered offensive to classify a female's or a child's role or ownership under that of the male or the elder by putting only one name into the possessive. Check your facts before writing *Mr. and Mrs. Haverford's business.* It might be that the Haverfords prefer *Dee Haverford's and Jim Haverford's business,* which gives them equal billing. *See also* PERSONAL PRONOUNS.

Precise language
    See CLARITY.

Predicate
    The predicate is everything in a sentence that is not the subject. In the following sentences, the predicate is underlined: *Quantum mechanics <u>is a subject about which I know little;</u> I <u>opened the present;</u> Knowing a little about a lot <u>is worse than knowing a lot about a little</u>.* The predicate must agree with the subject in number and person. If the subject is singular, the predicate must also be singular: *One of the ways I forget my*

worries is to take a hot bath. The subject is *one,* clearly singular, so the predicate verb, *is,* must also be singular. In cases such as these, be sure not to confuse *worries,* a plural noun, with *one,* the subject of the sentence.

Present tense

See TENSE: PAST, PRESENT, FUTURE.

Press release

Individuals and organizations put out press releases in order to publicize a message that will serve their needs. Newspapers, magazines, bulletins, and trade journals, among others, use press releases in a number of ways. In order to write a successful press release, you need to understand the differing interests and perspectives between the party issuing the press release and the party publishing it.

If you send a press release to a local newspaper, there are several things that might happen. It could be printed verbatim, paraphrased as a separate news item, or quoted as part of a larger news story. Of course, for the press release to be used at all, it must be perceived by the person you are sending it to as interesting and newsworthy.

Often a press release is simply a statement by the head of an organization, in which case the news story is the statement: *Vince Peterson, Jr., CEO of Ultimatech International, announced yesterday his company's plans to merge with Worldwide Limited, Inc.* The rest of the release might provide some background, discuss the plans in detail, quote Vince Peterson, Jr., at some length, and even forestall some expected criticism by refuting it: *Some critics have raised questions about such a merger possibly violating federal antitrust laws, but executives from both companies are quick to point out that there is still plenty of competition from independent media sources.*

If the release is responding to an existing or breaking story, and you want your message to be included in the discussion of it, be sure to make your release interesting by using powerful imagery, poetic cadence, or a unique slant.

Pronoun

Words that represent specific nouns are called pronouns. The common pronouns come in many forms:

Personal:

Personal pronouns are used in place of specific things or people. *I, you, she, he, it, we,* and *they* are all personal pronouns.

Demonstrative:

Demonstrative pronouns indicate specific things or people and suggest their relationship to the speaker. *This, that,* and *those* are demonstrative pronouns.

Intensive:

Intensive pronouns add *-self* or *-selves* to emphasize the nouns they follow: *You yourself ought to know that.* Note that these forms are also reflexive pronouns.

Interrogative

Interrogative pronouns indicate questioning: *what, which,* and *who.*

Reciprocal:

These pronouns (each other, one another) are used with plural antecedents to indicate separate actions or conditions of each element of the antecedent: *The student teachers helped each other.*

Reflexive:

Like intensive pronouns, reflexive pronouns are formed by adding *-self* or *-selves* to the nouns they follow: *myself, yourself, himself, herself, itself, ourselves, yourselves, themselves.* These words indicate previously described action, and, unlike intensifiers, stand alone: *The cat groomed itself and its kitten.*

Relative:

The following pronouns are relative: *that, what, whatever, which, whichever, who,* and *whoever.* Relative pronouns link dependent clauses to the main parts of sentences and indicate the relationship between them: *I know the man in the flannel suit who is sitting by the window.*

See also PERSONAL PRONOUNS.

Proofreading

The process of reading over what has been written and correcting typographical and spelling errors. Do not rely on electronic spell checkers alone to find all of your mistakes. Proofread your work very carefully and even have a friend look at it to lend a fresh perspective.

Proofreading can save a great deal of embarrassment. You do not want to hand in a beautiful report with pages stapled in upside down or out of order. Never assume that the final product looks like you think it does. Printers run out of ink, computers malfunction, and people make mistakes. Remember, the quality of the package reflects the quality of the writing. Failure to proofread your work suggests a lack of concern.

Proper noun

See CAPITALIZATION; NOUN.

Proposal

When writing a proposal, you are trying to convince the reader that the course of action that you support meets his or her goals as well. To accomplish this task, you need to know what the reader's goals are. Once you have determined them, you can set about the task of putting your ideas down into words. A proposal usually contains the following elements:

Introduction:

The introductory paragraph of your proposal should clearly state your purpose, your suggestions and the reasons that they are in the best interest of the reader. You want to make what you are offering sound interesting and valuable, and entice your reader to learn more.

Content paragraph(s):

These paragraphs should contain details about the idea you are proposing. Some questions to bear in mind in this section of your proposal are: Who exactly am I targeting? What are their needs? Why do they need what I am offering? What can I do to convince them further? Be creative. Use quotes, statistics, and any other elements that might support your points.

Concluding paragraph:

The last paragraph of your proposal should pack as much punch as the first. At this point, your reader should be sold on your concept; you should merely reiterate your points and end on a strong concluding note.

Prose

A literary style differentiated from poetry by greater variety of rhythm and its association to the patterns of everyday speech.

Pun

The humorous use of a word in such a way as to suggest a different meaning, or the use of words having the same or nearly the same sound but different meanings. Example: *The undertaker was in grave danger of falling into the cemetery plot.* In this sentence, the word *grave* is a pun because the danger occurs near a cemetery plot.

Punctuation

Punctuation marks tell how various parts of sentences are related to one another, as well as to other sentences. The following is a list of punctuation marks standard to the English language.

Accents:

These marks appear above or below letters to indicate their pronunciation within a word. The English language does not contain any words with accents; however, it shows accents carried over from other languages, such as in the word *résumé*.

Apostrophe:

Apostrophes (') mark possessives and contractions: *The girl's pinwheel; Let's go.*

Asterisk:

The asterisk (*) is more of a typographical device to emphasize parts of lists, notes to a page, and the like, rather than a punctuation mark: *Here are the important elements: *self-confidence; *consideration of others. . . .*

Colon:

The colon (:) stands before and sharply sets off lists and dependent or independent phrases or clauses: *His point was this: the market is sagging.* The colon also separates hours and minutes: *The report will be issued at 3:00 sharp.*

Comma:

The comma (,) separates elements and marks borders between things: *The author wrote short stories, essays, and vignettes; The author sold a collection of short stories, moved to a twelve-acre farm, and began writing her first novel.* The commas in the examples link and mark borders between items in a list and two independent clauses, respectively.

Commas also appear in numbers greater than 999 that are not dates; in dates between days and years, as in *November 23, 1968;* and to set off titles and direct quotations: *Annabel Lee, D.V.M., said, "The raven will be all right."*

Dash:

The dash (—) is used to divide words or ideas, and usually sets something off in a sentence, such as an interjection: *Some of you—and you know who you are—have been abusing the coffee-break policy.*

Ellipsis:

The ellipsis (. . .) indicates the omission of words within a sentence (three periods) or at the end of a sentence (four periods) from quoted speech, or any incomplete statement, whether attributed to someone or not: *The reviewer stated: In my opinion, this is . . . one of the greatest works of scholarship in the last ten years. . . .*

Exclamation Point:

The exclamation point (!) marks an emphatic statement: *Watch the cat in the road!*

Hyphen:

The hyphen (-) joins two words to form a compound word: *Anna claims that mass-produced clothes never fit her properly.*

Parentheses:

Parentheses [( )] are used to offset interjections or phrases inserted for the purpose of further explanation: *Each of the countries (Korea, Japan, and Vietnam) signed the pact.* When the phrase is intended to have greater importance, commas or dashes may be used instead.

Period:

The period (.) usually marks the end of a sentence: *This is a call to all my lost assignations.*

Question mark:

This punctuation ends an interrogatory sentence: *Where are you going this evening?*

Quotation marks:

Quotation marks ("")surround a single quote: *Mary said, "I've tried all possible avenues."* Quotation marks around single words or phrases are also used to indicate quotes within quotes, or that they are somehow in question: *"The little boy cried 'Wolf!' "*

Semicolon:

The semicolon (;) functions somewhat like the comma, but it is used to more clearly mark the distinctions between phrases or clauses that already contain commas: *She photographed sheep, cows, and other cattle grazing in the hills; panoramic vistas; and close-ups of pansies, bluebells, and morning glories; then she went to the bed and breakfast, where she received the news of her brother's marriage.*

See also APOSTROPHE; COLON; COMMA; DASH; ELLIPSIS; HYPHEN; PARENTHESES; QUOTATIONS; *and* SEMICOLON.

Purpose

When you begin work on a writing assignment, consider the following: Why are you writing? What do you want a particular piece to accomplish? These questions are fundamental in the writing process. If you are clear about your intentions before you begin, your work will be stronger and more focused. For example, if you are writing a cover letter for a résumé with the intent of getting a job interview, your purpose is to highlight those aspects of your background that present you as the most qualified candidate for the job. If you write a newspaper editorial to put forth the view that handguns should be outlawed, then the piece should only reflect points supporting that point of view. Having a purpose prevents digression, which would cause your readers to lose interest or become confused.

Question

See INTERROGATIVE SENTENCE.

Question mark

See INTERROGATIVE SENTENCE.

Quotation

Like questions, quotations come in two basic kinds—direct (*"That's okay,"* Mabel sighed) and indirect (*Obviously, I said that dinner was going to be late*). Note the differences in their punctuation and word order. Direct quotations are surrounded by quotation marks; indirect quotations are not, as they restate or report statements rather than reproducing them verbatim. Indirect quotations do not include punctuation to indicate the nature of the quoted sentence, and usually include words such as *said that* or *stated that*.

R

Racial, ethnic, and religious terms

Although stereotypical racial slurs are embedded in our language *(Indian giver)*, they should never be incorporated into your writing or speech. If you need to refer to people of a certain race or ethnic background, use the name that they would like you to use. The following list should give you an idea about the types of terms that are acceptable today.

Nationality/Ethnic Background	*Accepted Terms*
Americans of African descent	*African Americans, black people* (*Afro-American,* and *Negro* are no longer accepted)
People of Asian descent	*Asian Americans* (not *Oriental people*) or names denoting specific countries: *Japanese people, Chinese people, Korean people, etc.*
People of Central American descent	*Latina* (feminine) or *Latino* (masculine)
People of India	*Indians*
Inhabitants of Israel	*Israelis* (people who live in Israel are not necessarily Jewish)
People of the Jewish faith	*Jews* or *Jewish people*
Descendants of North America's original inhabitants	*Native Americans* (*Indian* is not accepted)

rather

Can be used as a qualifier *(it is rather chilly)* or as a subordinating conjunction *(I would rather not go to the top of the mountain)*. As a qualifier, *rather* adds only vagueness and ambiguity to your sentence. Use a more descriptive word like *somewhat, very*, or *slightly*.

reason is because

This is redundant and incorrect. *Reason* means *cause,* so to repeat the word *because* is unnecessary. Use the construction *reason is that: The reason I am late is that my cat ran up a tree. See also* BECAUSE OF VS. DUE TO ; REDUNDANCY.

Redundancy

Unnecessary repetition of words, phrases, or ideas. Redundancy detracts from the overall quality of your writing; try to rephrase or rewrite sentences that repeat ideas. Some redundant phrases to avoid: *old adage; repeat again; more better; revert back; round circle; trite cliché*. In the following redundant sentence, the unnecessary parts have been underlined: *Untrained pets <u>that haven't been housebroken</u> are difficult to handle <u>and tough to live with</u>*.

references

See CITATION.

Reflexive pronoun

A pronoun that contains the ending *-self* or *-selves* and amplifies the noun to which it refers: *myself, yourself, himself, herself, itself, ourselves, yourselves, themselves. See also* INTENSIVE PRONOUN.

Relative pronoun

See PRONOUN.

Religious terms

See RACIAL, ETHNIC, AND RELIGIOUS TERMS.

Repetition

See REDUNDANCY.

Report

The purpose of a report is to present information on a given topic. As opposed to an essay or an analysis, a report only conveys information without expressing opinions or speculation. Whether you are writing a high school book report, a college research report, or a professional business report, your purpose is similar: to survey, organize, and objectively present pertinent information. First, introduce your topic with a substantial paragraph of summary that indicates what can be found in subsequent paragraphs. The body of the report should present the detailed information organized into logical paragraphs. Your conclusion should restate the purpose or the main idea of the report and contain a few sentences of summary.

Research paper

See EXPOSITORY WRITING; LIBRARY RESEARCH.

Resignation, letter of

See BUSINESS LETTER.

Résumés and cover letters

The purpose of a résumé and its accompanying cover letter is to obtain an interview for a job position. Each needs to be well written and nicely presented. A cover letter is essentially a business letter that you write to sell yourself to the reader; you need to point out some of your strong "selling" points and sound like a self-assured, confident prospective employee. Here is a sample cover letter:

Brian Webb
300 W. 87th Street, #4
New York, NY 10000
(212) 437–8968

October 4, 1996

Ms. Mary Mack
The Red Balloon Marketing Firm
661 East End Ave.
New York, NY 10000

Dear Ms. Mack:

I am responding to the advertisement placed by your company in the October 3 *New York Times*. I feel that I am a strong candidate for the Marketing Assistant position being offered at The Red Balloon Marketing Firm.

As you can see from my résumé, I am a highly motivated person who performs well in the workplace. I have had two opportunities to work in marketing: one as an intern at a small architectural firm; and one as an assistant to a senior marketing executive at a book publishing company. With several months' experience, I feel certain that my interests, abilities, and aspirations are well suited to a career in marketing. It is for this reason that I am applying for a position at your company.

Please refer to the enclosed résumé. I look forward to hearing from you about setting up an interview.

Sincerely,

[INSERT SIGNATURE]

Brian Webb

The opening sentence is essentially a personal introduction presenting you to the reader: State your purpose for writing and mention where you heard about the job opening. The body paragraph(s) should highlight two or three of your most relevant experiences, or explain why you think you're a good candidate. Don't go into too much detail—let your résumé speak for itself. To avoid repetition, don't use the same language in your cover letter that you use in your résumé. In closing, mention a time or day that you will call to follow up, or give the reader some idea of when you want to hear a response.

A résumé comprises three major sections: educational background, professional or relevant experience, and activities or personal interests. The education and experience sections should be arranged chronologically beginning with the most recent. Include awards and scholarships in the education section; list achievements, publications, courses given, and professional affiliations in the experience section. You may or may not choose to write "References Available Upon Request" at the bottom of your résumé. This has traditionally been standard, but is now often regarded as empty filler information. You may assume that the employer will notify you if he or she wants to see your list of references. Following is a sample résumé:

BRIAN WEBB
300 W. 87th Street, #4
New York, NY 10000
(212) 437–8968

Education
B.A. in Accounting, The University of North Carolina at Chapel Hill, 1990–1994
Junior semester abroad: The University of Wales at Bangor, 1993
Summer courses in accounting at Milliken College, Summer 1991

Experience
<u>Marketing Assistant</u>
The Lexington Press, Inc., Boston, MA , 1994–1995
    Assistant to the senior marketing coordinator at a book publishing company. Set up marketing plans to help publicize top-selling books in large book superstores; verified publicity release dates and coordinated marketing projects with the publicity and sales departments. Kept records and organized the filing system for the entire department.
<u>Marketing Assistant Internship</u>
Stracher and Sons, Inc., Raleigh, NC , Fall 1992
    Worked with the two members of the marketing staff at a small, competitive architectural office. Participated in clerical duties such as faxing, filing, photocopying, and answering phones. Helped to compile information that was used by

the marketing director to write job proposals.

Career Counseling Office Assistant

University of North Carolina at Chapel Hill Career Office, Academic years 1992–1994

Worked in the Career Counseling Office as a part-time job. Scheduled student appointments; filed and organized counselors' records; distributed fliers and worked on campus mailing projects. Chosen by the staff of counselors to deliver a speech to the senior class.

Activities

Co-captain of the UNC–CH Ski Team

Student government: Junior class treasurer

Performance art: instructor and performer with the Chapel Hill Troupers

Community service: tutor for high school students

Dog Walkers, Inc.: pet care volunteer

Most entry-level candidate résumés should be one page long; people with established careers may have multiple-page résumés. If you need to shorten yours, tailor the résumé for the potential employer by revealing only your most pertinent and impressive qualities. Check for typos, spelling mistakes, and poor grammar; you can never be too careful with details. Some employers automatically eliminate any candidate who submits a cover letter or résumé containing careless errors.

Revising

See DRAFTS.

Rewriting

See DRAFTS.

Rhetoric

The arrangement of ideas in writing or speech to achieve your purpose in addressing your audience. Rhetoric relies upon strong language and meticulously organized patterns of argument, logic, and persuasion.

Rhetorical question

A question posed simply to achieve an effect, not to obtain an answer: *How can we work together to achieve our goals? The answer is clear: we unite, we picket, we protest.* The author of this statement does not expect an answer from her readers. Rather, she uses the question to set up a delivery for her message.

Ridicule

A derisive tone directed at the reader or the subject of a piece of writing. Avoid making fun of people or institutions in your writing. If your goal is satire, be sure not to sound aggressive or nasty; to do so is to defeat the subtlety and humor of satire. Ridicule should be used sparingly, if at all, and should be monitored carefully to avoid insults and malice. *See also* SATIRE.

Run-on sentence

A poorly punctuated sentence containing more than one independent clause (a group of words that formulates a complete thought and contains at least a subject and verb). Run-on sentences are usually the result of comma splices—commas used to join independent clauses. Do not use commas for this purpose. Use a semi-colon or break the clauses apart with a period. Occasionally, you can use a comma with one of these coordinating conjunctions: *and, so, yet, but, or, nor.* Here is a run-on sentence: *The sun rose over the mountain, it was a beautiful morning.* Rewrite as one of the following: *The sun rose over the mountain. It was a beautiful morning.* Or: *The sun rose over the mountain; it was a beautiful morning.* Or: *The sun rose over the mountain, and it was a beautiful morning.*

S

Salutation

A greeting at the beginning of a letter: *Dear Ms. Jameson; To Whom It May Concern; To the Manager. See also* BUSINESS LETTER; PERSONAL LETTER.

Satire

A style of writing in which the writer mocks human vices and follies. A tone of sarcasm, humor, and scorn characterizes satirical literature. It is possible to satirize your subject without brutally attacking it. Use good taste, refinement, and enough humor to signify that your remarks are not intended to cause the ruin or devastation of your subject or to better yourself by degrading others. Satire is just to poke fun. *See also* RIDICULE.

say vs. *go*

See GO VS. SAY.

Second person

See POINT OF VIEW.

Semantics

In literary criticism, the study of the meanings of words, symbols, and signs.

Semicolon

Semicolons (;) are used to separate two independent clauses (*Our cat likes to eat cat food; the dog eats filet mignon*). The semicolon is stronger than a comma and weaker than a period. Remember, commas should never be used to separate two independent clauses without an appropriate conjunction (*and, but,* etc.); the proper way to do so is with a semicolon, a comma with a coordinating conjunction, or a period. A semicolon can be used with or without a conjunction, depending on the tone of your sentence: *The band's lead singer prefers slow ballads; however, the drummer loves to play fast dance songs.* The other use of the semicolon is to separate items in a list. Note: Use a semicolon only when the elements in the list are several words in length each, or when there are commas within elements: *These are a few of my favorite things: raindrops on roses; whiskers on kittens; brown paper packages tied up with string.* You can use commas instead of semicolons to separate elements of a list when they are single-word items: *Common traits among inmates include: lunacy, mayhem, absurdity, and hilarity. I need to buy hot dogs, ketchup, and chips from the grocery store; apples and oranges from the fruit stand; and pens and stationery from the paper-goods store.* The semicolons in the latter two examples separate dependent (not independent) clauses. *See also* LIST; RUN-ON SENTENCE.

Sentence

A group of words that includes a subject and verb and expresses a complete thought. Sentence structure is governed by the rules of grammar. Complete sentences are the basic building blocks of writing. *See also* RUN-ON SENTENCE; SENTENCE FRAGMENT.

Sentence fragment

An incomplete sentence. It may lack a verb or a subject, or it may be a dependent clause (which is not capable of standing alone). Some fragments: *the man on the street corner* (no verb); *going to the movies* (no subject); *since we have been in Los Angeles* (dependent clause). You could make complete sentences out of these examples by adding the proper sentence parts: *The man on the street corner looks suspicious; I am going to the movies; Since we have been in Los Angeles, it has been incredibly hot;* Commands such as *Come here* and *Let's eat lunch* are not fragments because the implied subject is *you,* making the sentence complete with verb and subject. There are some acceptable uses for fragments: exclamations *(Oh, my gosh!),* some questions *(Where to? What now?),* and some informal transitions *(One last remark. Now for the punch line.).*

several vs. a few

These may refer to the same amount *(several people* [6] *came to the picnic; a few people* [6] *came to the picnic),* but the difference is in the tone. *Several* suggests that the amount indicated is considerably large, while *a few* suggests that the amount is negligible or smaller than desired.

Sexist language

Any words, phrases, sentence structures, or underlying ideas that discriminate against one gender or glorify the other gender are considered sexist language. Sexist language is offensive; you should avoid it in your writing. The English language contains many inherent sexist references such as the "generic he" pronoun; the term *man* that traditionally refers to the entire human race; the male form of address *Mr.,* which, unlike *Mrs.* and *Miss,* does not disclose marital status; and even the word *women,* which some argue is a diminutive derivation of the root word *men.* Fortunately, the language is evolving into a more gender-neutral or nonsexist form of expression. Today, we have nonsexist word choices: *he or she; humankind; Mr. and Ms.; womyn.*

In terms of pronouns, *he or she* or plain *she* are accepted when gender is not known. You may write: *A good doctor cares about her patients* or *A good doctor cares about her or his patients.* Or, better yet, eliminate the need to specify the gender of the subject by pluralizing it: *Good doctors care about their patients.* Another way to avoid specifying the subject's gender is to rewrite, and replace references with synonymous words. Compare these sentences: *Even when doctors go home to their wives and children, they don't stop caring for their patients. Even when doctors go home to their families, they don't stop caring for their patients.*

Eliminate from your writing all words that assume male-only professions: use *chairperson,* not *chairman; firefighter,* not *fireman; worker's* compensation, not *workman's; postal worker,* not *mailman.* By the same token, avoid implications that women are meant to do certain jobs: *waitress; stewardess;*

typist; secretary; nurse; babysitter. Men and women are equally capable of performing every job and your writing should reflect that.

It is offensive to use gender epithets such as *woman doctor* or *female professor;* such terms imply that doctors or professors are male unless otherwise specified. By the same token, never assume that *secretaries, nurses,* or *babysitters* are women. Also, do not refer to people over the age of sixteen as *girls* or *boys.* These terms belittle people who should be called *women* and *men. Ladies* and *gentlemen* have old-fashioned and sometimes sexist connotations as well. Not all women are ladies, nor are all men gentlemen—the terms are outdated socioeconomic labels. *See also* GENDER.

Sexual orientation

If it is necessary to refer to somebody's sexual preference in your writing, use words that will not offend any readers. The most widely accepted terms for homosexual people are *gay* and *lesbian.* Some words like *queer* or *queen* are used by gay organizations (The Queer Nation is one such group). Still, use the term *queer* very carefully—it also has negative connotations. Drag queens use the term *queen* to refer to themselves, but again, be careful of the context in which you use it. *Gay* often refers to male homosexuals, but can also refer to female homosexuals. Often, however, homosexual women prefer being called *lesbians,* not *gay people.* Find out which word your audience accepts. Refer to all sexual orientations with respect and equality. *and See also* GENDER; RACIAL, ETHNIC, *and* RELIGIOUS TERMS; *and* SEXIST LANGUAGE.

shall vs. *will*

Shall is used primarily in questions to express opinion or consent: *Shall we leave now? Shall* can also be used to produce a formal tone: *We shall leave the gathering at your convenience.* Otherwise, *will* is preferable when stating a future event or asking a question: *The eclipse will occur at 4:07 p.m.; Will you be present at the gathering?*

Similar words

See CONFUSED WORDS; HOMONYMS; HOMOPHONES; *and* SYNONYMS.

Simile

A figure of speech that compares two things using *like* or *as: Nathan dances like a fool; The child streaked the dinner party, naked as a jaybird. See also* METAPHOR.

Slang

Nonstandard English, usually resulting from lazy diction or jargon. Vivid, useful slang has the potential to unite sub-cultures (such as groups of technicians, gangs, teenagers, etc.), but it also has a tendency to sound flippant, disrespectful to authority, and imprecise. Slang: *The kids were chowing down at Micky D.'s.* Revised: *The children were eating at McDonald's.* Avoid slang in formal writing. When using it in informal writing, know your audience. *See also* JARGON.

Slash

A diagonal symbol (/) used between options and to separate lines of poetry or musical lyrics that are run in to the text. Options: *Check the positive/negative feedback monitor; I am taking World Music pass/fail; Karen received an A–/B+ on her paper.* Musical lyrics written out as text: *"Mary had a little lamb/little lamb/little lamb. . . . "*

so

A coordinating conjunction that, along with a comma, can join together two independent clauses *(Eric wants to leave early, so we should allow him to perform first),* and also an intensifier that amplifies the meaning of an adjective or adverb *(The Red Sox played so well last night).* Avoid using *so* as an intensifier. It is weak and nondescriptive, and forms an incomplete comparison when not followed by *that.* You must complete the comparison: *The Red Sox played so well last night that I'm glad I went to the game. See also* INCOMPLETE COMPARISON.

Speech

See ORAL PRESENTATION.

Split infinitive

Inserting a word between *to* and its verb: *to sweetly sing; to faithfully follow*. Strictly speaking, infinitives are not to be split; however, sometimes it is necessary to do so, either to preserve meaning or to avoid awkwardness. The famous *Star Trek* motto, *To boldly go where no one has gone before*, would suffer if the words were rearranged: *To go boldly where no one has gone before; Boldly to go where no one has gone before; To go where no one has boldly gone before*. None sounds as good as the original. As a general guideline, however, avoid splitting infinitives unless doing so weakens your intent. *See also* VERB.

Squinting modifier

An ambiguously placed modifier. A modifier is any word or phrase that explains a noun, verb, or other phrase. In the following sentence, the word *often* is a squinting modifier: *Reading Chaucer's poetry often is a difficult task*. Does the author mean *Reading Chaucer's poetry is often a difficult task*, or *Reading Chaucer's poetry on a regular basis is a difficult task*? Place descriptive phrases in logical locations within your sentences. *See also* DANGLING MODIFIER; MISPLACED MODIFIER.

Sr.

See JR. AND SR.

Subject

One of the basic components of a sentence. The subject indicates who or what the sentence is about. Simple subjects are nouns or pronouns: *The sun rises; In the show, the woman wears a wig; I am a terrible bowler; They need an insurance policy; Happiness makes the world go round*.

Complete subjects are simple subjects plus all of their modifiers (adjectives and adverbs): *The way you look is beyond compare*; <u>*The men and women who keep our neighborhoods safe*</u> *deserve many thanks.*

Subjective case
See CASE: SUBJECTIVE, OBJECTIVE, POSSESSIVE.

Subject/verb agreement
See AGREEMENT.

Subjunctive mood
See MOOD: INDICATIVE, IMPERATIVE, SUBJUNCTIVE.

Superlative
An adjective or adverb form that describes the best or the most extreme: *fastest; prettiest; bluest.* Usually, you can form the superlative by adding *-est* to the end of an adjective or adverb. However, this is not true for some words, especially longer adjectives, which must take *most*: *most careful; most talented. See also* COMPARATIVE.

Synonyms
Words that have similar or identical meanings: *big, giant, vast, enormous, sizeable, great, substantial; talk, communicate, discuss, speak.* You need a good thesaurus to look up useful and accurate synonyms. A strong vocabulary is an indispensable writing tool, and synonyms are a good way to begin expanding your repertoire of words. Why write about a fun summer vacation when you could describe your rollicking, jocular summer antics? On the same note, however, remember that it is best to use words that convey the proper meaning based on context. Never use a big word in place of a simple word just to raise your reader's opinion of you. If you are describing an offensive insult your brother made, don't glorify it by calling it a censorious castigation.

Syntax
The way words are put together in sentences and other structured word patterns, such as phrases and clauses. Grammar

(the rules) governs syntax (the structure). English language syntax, in its most reductionist state, is based upon the structure of sentences—verbs following subjects, modifiers placed after verbs. Naturally, the flow and expression of language requires variations and modifications to this structure. Proper syntax can accommodate many different types of sentence structures.

T

Tables and charts

Information arranged in a straightforward, tabulated order can be inserted into most word-processing documents. For example:

GUIDE TO COLLEGES, VOLS. 1–6 PUBLISHING SCHEDULE

TITLE	First Draft Due	Second Draft Due	Final Complete MS
Vol. 1, Northeast	2/1/94	5/1/94	8/1/94
Vol. 2, Southeast	3/1/94	6/1/94	9/1/94
Vol. 3, Midwest	4/1/94	7/1/94	10/1/94
Vol. 4, Northwest	5/15/94	7/15/94	10/30/94
Vol. 5, Southwest	6/15/94	8/15/94	11/15/94
Vol. 6, Index of Programs	7/1/95	8/1/95	10/1/95

Note that there is a descriptive title at the top of the table, the columns are labeled along the top, and the rows are labeled along the left side. The information presented in the table is consistent in format and quick and easy to read. If you insert tables or charts into your work, be certain that they are important. If something is better explained in words and sentences, don't create a table unnecessarily.

Tense: past, present, future

The verb tense you choose to write in affects the tone of your piece. Write in the past tense, including the past perfect and past progressive, for events that have occurred prior to the present: *Jasmine went to school. She was going to make a stop at the park, but then she decided not to.* Also, most fictional narratives are presented in the past tense. Use the present tense, including the present perfect and present progressive, to write about actions in progress, general truths, literature, and paraphrased ideas: *I am looking for that file; Jane Eyre becomes a French teacher; People like to feel useful;* Use the future tense, future perfect and future progressive, to foretell events that have not yet occurred: *You will like what you see.* It is very important that you never shift tenses unintentionally within a work; if you do, you cause the reader to become confused.

Term paper

See EXPOSITORY WRITING; LIBRARY RESEARCH; *and* RESEARCH PAPER.

than vs. *then*

Than is a conjunction that shows a comparison between two things: *The air is cooler in the shade than it is in direct sunlight. Then* is an adverb that signifies time: *The air is cool in the morning, then it warms up by the afternoon.*

Thank-you note

A short, polite letter thanking somebody for a gift, favor, etc. As with all letters, know your audience and write accordingly. Tell the reader that you appreciate the kind thought, perhaps include a short anecdote or some news that may be of interest, and close with an affectionate or polite ending:

December 30, 1995

Dear Aunt Mabel,

Thank you very much for the thoughtful Christmas gift. I love the slippers; they match my new bathrobe perfectly. Those bunny ears drive my puppy crazy! Have a Happy New Year.

Love,

Lisa

---

that vs. which

Both are used to begin dependent clauses, but *that* presents restrictive clauses (referring to specific things) and *which* presents nonrestrictive clauses (referring to something that is not essential to the main idea). Compare: *The horse that you rode on is galloping away; Those Tuesday night programs, which I particularly dislike, are going to be aired on Wednesday nights now.*

the fact is

More often than not, this statement can be eliminated from your writing without affecting the meaning in any way. Note the difference: *Although I promised to spend the weekend at my sister-in-law's apartment, the fact is I would rather not go; Although I promised to spend the weekend at my sister-in-law's apartment, I would rather not go.* The phrase *the fact is* wastes words and often works negatively to make the writer look uncertain about the facts being presented. *See also* CIRCUMLOCUTION.

then

See THAN VS. THEN.

Thesis

See EXPOSITORY WRITING; LIBRARY RESEARCH; *and* RESEARCH PAPER.

Third person

See POINT OF VIEW.

Title

The title of your piece should be informative, descriptive, and intriguing. It should call the reader's attention to the theme of your work and draw the reader in using interesting words. Put the title at the top of your first page. Do not use quotation marks around your own title, but be sure to properly italicize titles of other authors' works that you mention within the title. As with all types of writing, know your audience. Create a title that will serve their needs and expectations. If you have written a college essay comparing two works of literature, title the piece appropriately *(The Abandoned Child:* Bleak House, David Copperfield, *and the Theme of Victorian Orphans in Dickens' Novels)*. You wouldn't title an essay like this *Going Solo*—it sounds flippant and gives no indication of the scope of your essay. On the other hand, if you're writing for a fashion magazine or other entertainment publication, create a title that sounds fun, pleasing, and enlightening.

Titles of works

See CAPITALIZATION; TITLE.

Tone

The way you choose to present your attitude, mood, and level of formality in a piece of writing. Writing style can be personal or formal, sympathetic or satiric, chatty, cheerful, haughty, derisive, stiff or loose, tragic or joyful, academic or entertaining, and so on. You must accomplish with words alone what you ordinarily accomplish in face-to-face conversation using not only words, but also body language, facial expression, and the tone of your voice. Know your audience. If you have been selected to write a pamphlet for junior-high-school students about the harmful effects of smoking, keep your tone informative, authoritative, somewhat formal, and instructive: *Smoking has been proven to cause lung cancer in 40 percent of all long-term smokers. The smartest way to prevent yourself from becoming part of this deadly statistic is to say no to smoking at a young age.* In this example, a certain amount of informality exists because of the second-person address *(you),* but the overall tone is sober and foreboding. Conversely, if you are writing an e-mail message to your friend from college, you could get away with informality and chumminess: *Hey! What's going on? I thought I'd write you a quick note to see how you're doing.*

Topic sentence

The sentence in a paragraph that conveys the main idea. Since by definition a paragraph is a set of sentences that makes a statement and then develops its central idea, every paragraph you write should include a topic sentence. Organizationally, this system makes perfect sense. If you locate two topic sentences in one of your paragraphs, ask yourself whether the paragraph might benefit from being broken up into two more fully developed paragraphs, each containing its own topic sentence and supporting ideas. When you learned how to take notes for school or to read others' work critically, you were probably taught to develop an eye for locating the topic sentence. In your own writing, use that same skill. Identify your topic sentence to help you keep track of what is central and what is secondary to the topic idea.

toward vs. *towards*

In the U.S., *toward* is more acceptable than *towards*, which prevails in Great Britain: *Don't steer the boat toward the water skier.*

Trademark

See GENERIC TERM VS. TRADEMARK.

Transitional phrase

A word or group of words that serves to link two discrete ideas, sentences, or independent clauses: *however, but, on the other hand, still, instead, yet, additionally, moreover, therefore, perhaps, consequently, subsequently, for example, although.* An essential component of good writing is knowing how to make connections between ideas. If you have trouble linking your sentences, the piece will seem choppy and unpolished. Reread your work to make sure that each thought flows logically into the next. If it doesn't, insert an explanatory word or two to show the relationship between ideas. Note the difference:

> *Ron and Joe wanted to place bets on the racehorses. They don't earn very much money at their summer jobs.*

> *Ron and Joe wanted to place bets on the racehorses. Unfortunately, however, they don't earn very much money at their summer jobs.*

Use commas to set off the transitional phrases, particularly conjunctions (*and, but,* etc.). If you find it impossible to identify the relationship, chances are your argument or logic won't make sense to your reader either. Rewrite until the only ideas expressed in your writing are those that are relevant to the piece as a whole.

Transitional sentence

Transitional sentences explain the relationship between ideas and paragraphs. Here are two sentences in need of a transition: *Some chefs insist that sherbet be served to the people for whom they are preparing a gourmet meal. The food tastes better, the flavors are enhanced, and people are more prepared to enjoy the next course.* Here are the same ideas with transitions that better explain the relationship between the ideas: *Some chefs insist that sherbet be served to the people for whom they are preparing a gourmet meal. Sherbet clears the palate by eliminating salty and bitter aftertastes left over from the meal's first courses. After sherbet, chefs claim, the food tastes better, the flavors are enhanced, and people are more prepared to enjoy the next course.* See also TRANSITIONAL PHRASE.

try and vs. try to

Try and is an idiomatic expression meaning *try to*: *Just try and stop me.* The grammatically correct construction is *try to,* which should be used in all formal writing: *Let's try to go to the community picnic.*

U

Underlining

See ITALICS.

uninterested

See DISINTERESTED VS. UNINTERESTED.

unique

Unique is a modifier that, strictly speaking, is absolute and cannot be modified itself. Since *unique* means *one of a kind,* it makes no sense to speak of something being *pretty unique* or *very unique;* it is either one of a kind or it isn't.

upon vs. on

See ON VS. UPON.

V

've vs. of

See OF VS. 'VE.

Viewpoint

See POINT OF VIEW.

Verb

A verb is part of speech that expresses action or a state of being. In the following sentences, the verbs are underlined: *I ate the last piece of apple strudel; Running is a good exercise for those who stick to it faithfully; Brett seemed shaken by the news; Unlike previous generations, the current crop of youngsters takes the fact that all life on earth is interconnected for granted.*

Some sentences have more than one verb. Verbs can be transitive, which means they take direct objects: *The bat hit the ball; Smadar earns her living by writing.* Other verbs are intransitive, which means they do not take direct objects: *Grieta laughed at my proposal; Everyone wondered what you meant by that; Reading is fundamental.* This last example is a specific type of intransitive verb: a linking verb. Linking verbs connect subjects with predicates. Here are some common linking verbs: *be, am, are, is, was, were, look, grow, seem, appear, smell, feel, become, act.*

Helping verbs can include *be* and its related forms, and words like *must* and *might: I will be going as soon as my bus arrives; Many students could not solve the problem.*

Verbs must agree with their subjects in number. A singular subject must take a singular verb; a plural subject must take a plural verb. The tense of a verb indicates whether the action is taking place in the past, present, future, or some combination of these. For example, the past imperfect involves action that began at some indefinite time in the past and has not yet ended: *He has been teaching in Philadelphia for many years.* The past perfect involves action that began and ended in the indefinite past: *The big oil companies had deforested much of Central America before international pressure forced them to change their ways.*

Active verbs indicate that the subject is the agent of action, while passive verbs show that the subject is being "done to." Active: *Hemingway wrote* For Whom the Bell Tolls. Passive:

For Whom the Bell Tolls *was written by Hemingway.* Generally, the active voice provides more vigor than the passive, although there are times when the passive voice is preferred. *See also* VOICE: ACTIVE, PASSIVE.

very

An overused modifier. *See also* LITTLE.

Voice: active, passive

Verbs can change in form to expres two voices, the active voice and the passive voice. Voice indicates whether the subject of the verb performs or receives the action described by the verb, and also determines the mood and tone of a piece of writing. If the subject of the sentence performs the action, the sentence is in the active voice. If the subject receives the action, the sentence is in the passive voice. In the following two examples, note whether the subject is performing or receiving the verb's action: *Mario gave the ticket to the attendant; The ticket was given to the attendant by Mario.* In the first sentence, the subject, *Mario,* actively completes a specific deed. In the second, the subject, *ticket,* passively receives the action. The second example, written in the passive voice, sounds roundabout and awkward, particularly when compared with the first. A general guideline is to avoid the passive voice and rephrase your sentences to use the active voice whenever possible. Grammatically, the passive voice is just as correct as the active. Stylistically, however, the active voice communicates ideas much more clearly and smoothly.

The passive voice may be used appropriately when the subject of the sentence is unimportant or indefinite. Here is an example of a passive sentence in which the subject is indefinite: *The musical was choreographed beautifully.* In this sentence, since the name of the choreographer is not mentioned, one may assume that it is either unknown or unimportant to the central idea. As a basic rule of thumb, use the active voice unless there is a good reason for using the passive. Know the difference and choose your voice discern-ingly.

W

well vs. good
See GOOD VS. WELL.

whether . . . or
See CORRELATIVE CONJUNCTION.

which
See THAT VS. WHICH.

who vs. whom
A dilemma that commonly faces writers is when to use *who* and when to use *whom*. Remember that *who* is always a sub-ject, and *whom* is always an object. Another trick for remem-bering which word to choose is to check for prepositions. If a preposition such as *for, to, with,* or *under* precedes the place where *who* or *whom* should go, the choice is *whom: To whom do I make out the check? Do not ask for whom the bell tolls. With whom will we dine this evening?*

When the preposition and the pronoun are separated in the sentence, it is becoming increasingly acceptable, both in speech and formal writing, to use the subjective case: *Who do I make the check out to? Who is the bell tolling for? Who are we dining with this evening? Whom* is still correct, and by many, preferred in these sentences.

Do not use *whom* when the pronoun is the subject of a de-pendent clause, even if it follows a preposition. WRONG: *I will go to the party with whomever asks me first.* RIGHT: *I will go to the party with whoever asks me first.* In these cases, the phrase *whoever asks me first* acts as a single noun in the objective case; within the phrase itself, however, the pronoun *whoever* is the subject.

One method that often makes clear which of the two options is correct is to replace them in the sentence with a personal pronoun: *her* or *him* for *whom,* or *she* or *he* for *who: Who[m] may I say is calling? She . . . is calling* or *Her . . . is calling?* If *she,* then *who;* if *her,* then *whom.*

whose vs. who's

If you can replace either word in a sentence with *who is,* then the correct choice is *who's: Who's coming to dinner? Who is coming to dinner?* If the sense is possessive, then the correct choice is *whose: Whose plate is this?*

will

See SHALL VS. WILL.

-wise

A suffix that usually means *regarding.* It can be added to any noun to create an adverb, and often represents poor style: *Computerwise, I don't have a clue; We are in bad shape moneywise.* Avoid this construction as much as possible in your writing.

Word choice

Using the right words makes the crucial difference between a compelling, effective piece of writing and a confusing, unintelligible one. *See also* CLARITY.

Wordiness

See CONCISENESS.

Y

YOU'RE VS. YOUR

If you can replace either word in a sentence with *you are*, then the correct choice is *you're: You're a fool; You are a fool*. If the sense is possessive, then the correct choice is *your: Your chair is broken*.

STYLE
Quick-Finder

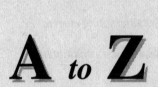

A *to* Z

A

ABA   Acronym for *American Bar Association*.

ABCs

ab init.   Abbreviation for the Latin term *ab initio*, meaning "from the beginning."

Aboriginal, Aborigine   Capitalize when referring to the indigenous people of Australia.

abr.   Abbreviation for *abridged*.

AC   Acronym for *alternating current*.

A/C   Abbreviation for *air conditioning*.

Achilles' heel

across-the-board   As an adjective.

A.D.   Abbreviation for the Latin term *anno Domini*, meaning "in the year of our Lord."

Adam's apple

ad hoc

adieu

ad-lib

ad nauseam

AF Acronym for *audio frequency.*

AFL–CIO Acronym for *American Federation of Labor and Congress of Industrial Organizations.*

African American Hyphenate only when using as an adjective.

AIDS Acronym for *Acquired Immunodeficiency Syndrome.*

air- Compound words beginning with *air-* are not usually hyphenated (e.g., *airport*).

a.k.a. Abbreviation for *also known as.*

Alabama Abbreviation *AL.*

Alaska Abbreviation *AK.*

Alberta Canadian province; abbreviation *AB.*

ALGOL Acronym for *algorithmic language;* a computer programming language.

all-or-nothing As an adjective.

alma mater

also-ran

Alzheimer's disease

a.m. or **A.M.** Abbreviation for the Latin term *ante meridiem,* meaning "before noon."

ambassador Capitalize only when using as a formal title preceding a name.(e.g., Ambassador Shelley).

amendment Capitalize only when referring to amendments of a specific document (e.g., *the Thirteenth Amendment to the Constitution*).

AMA Acronym for *American Medical Association.*

Amish

amp Abbreviation for *amperage, ampere,* or *amplifier.*

Anglo- Always capitalized.

anorexia nervosa

ante- Prefix meaning "before."

A-OK

a posteriori

Apostle's Creed

appt. Abbreviation for *appointment.*

APR Acronym for *annual percentage rate.*

April Fools' Day The first day in April.

a priori

apt. Abbreviation for *apartment.*

Aquarius A sign of the zodiac, (the Water Carrier); January 20–February 18.

arch- Compound words beginning with *arch-* are not usually hyphenated (e.g., *archbishop*).

archipelago

arctic   Capitalize only if part of a proper noun (e.g., *Arctic Circle*).

Aries   A sign of the zodiac, (the Ram); March 21–April 19.

Arizona   Abbreviation *AZ.*

Arkansas   Abbreviation *AK.*

ARM   Acronym for *adjustable rate mortgage.*

around-the-clock   As an adjective.

art deco or **Art Deco**

ASAP   Acronym for *as soon as possible.*

ASCII   Acronym for *American Standard Code of Information Interchange.*

assoc.   Abbreviation for *association.*

ATM   Acronym for *automated teller machine.*

atm.   Abbreviation for *atmosphere* or *atmospheric.*

attorney   Capitalize only when part of a title preceding or following a name (e.g., *District Attorney Richard Harris; Susan Browning, Attorney General*).

attn.   Abbreviation for *attention.*

auld lang syne

au naturel

au revoir

auto. Abbreviation for *automatic*.

auxiliary

avant-garde

-away Compound words ending in *-away* are not usually hyphenated (e.g., *hideaway*).

AWOL Acronym for *absent without leave*.

B

b. Abbreviation for *born*.

baccalaureate

back- Compound words beginning with *back-* are not usually hyphenated (e.g., *backbiting*), and are frequently spelled out as two words (e.g., *back door*). When in doubt, consult a dictionary.

back-to-back

bald-faced or **baldfaced**

ball-and-socket

Band-Aid Trademarked name for adhesive bandages.

bar-   Compound words beginning with *bar-* are not usually hyphenated (e.g., *barroom*).

bare-   Compound words beginning with *bare-* are not usually hyphenated (e.g., *bareknuckled*).

bar mitzvah

base-   Compound words beginning with *base-* are not usually hyphenated (e.g., *baseline*).

BASIC   Acronym for *Beginner's All-purpose Symbolic Instruction Code;* a computer language.

bas/bat mitzvah

battle-ax

B.C.   Abbreviation for *before Christ* (see entry in "Elements of Style A–Z").

B.C.E.   Abbreviation for *before the Common Era* (see entry in "Elements of Style A–Z").

bdrm.   Abbreviation for *bedroom.*

be-all

Beaufort scale

bed-and-breakfast or **B&B**

bell-bottoms

belles lettres

behind-the-scenes   As an adjective.

belt   Capitalize only if referring to a specific geographical region (e.g., *Corn Belt*).

best-   Compound words beginning with *best-* are usually hyphenated (e.g., *best-seller*).

bet. or **btwn.**   Abbreviations for *between*.

better-   Compound words beginning with *better-* are usually hyphenated when they appear before the noun they modify (e.g., *better-known musician*).

bi-   Compound words beginning with *bi-* are not usually hyphenated (e.g., *biennial*).

Bible   Capitalize only when referring to the Christian religious text.

bibl.   Abbreviation for *bibliography*.

big-   Compound words beginning with *big-* are not usually hyphenated (e.g., *bighearted*).

bill   Capitalize only when part of a proper noun (e.g., *Bill of Rights*).

bio-   Compound words beginning with *bio-* are not usually hyphenated (e.g., *biotechnology*).

bird's-eye

black-   Compound words beginning with *black-* are usually hyphenated; however, there are many exceptions (e.g., *blackberry; blacksmith; blacklist.*) When in doubt, consult a dictionary.

black-and-white   As an adjective.

black and white or **B&W**   As a noun.

blood-   Compound words beginning with *blood-* are usually hyphenated; however, there are many exceptions (e.g., *blood-curdling; bloodletting; bloodthirsty.*) When in doubt, consult a dictionary.

blue-   Compound words beginning with *blue-* are not usually hyphenated (e.g., *blueberry, bluegrass, blueprint*) except in phrases such as *blue-collar* or *blue-eyed.* When in doubt, consult a dictionary.

B'nai B'rith

-board   Compound words ending in *-board* are not usually hyphenated (e.g., *overboard*).

bold-faced

bombshell

bona fide

bon mot

bon vivant

Boolean

bookkeeper, bookkeeping

boomtown

Bordeaux; pl. Bordeaux

born-again   As an adjective.

bottom-line   As an adjective.

bottom line   As a noun.

-bound   Compound words ending in *-bound* are not usually hyphenated (e.g., *northbound*).

bourgeois   A lower- or middle-class individual.

bourgeoisie   The lower or middle class.

Braille

brain-   Compound words beginning with *brain-* are not usually hyphenated (e.g., *brainwash*).

brand-new

bread-and-butter   As an adjective.

British Columbia   Canadian province; abbreviation *BC*.

Briton   A native of Great Britain.

broad-minded

brokenhearted

Bronze Age

bu.   Abbreviation for *bushel*.

Buddhist

burnout

bwd. or **back.**   Abbreviation for *backward*.

by-and-by

Byzantine

c. Abbreviation for *copyright*.

C. Abbreviation for *Celsius*.

ca. Abbreviation for the Latin word *circa,* meaning "approximately" (e.g., *ca. 1917*).

cal. Abbreviation for *calorie*.

California Abbreviation *CA.*

call- Compound words beginning with *call-* are not usually hyphenated (e.g., *callback*).

calyx; pl. calyxes or calyces.

camouflage

campaign

can. or canc. Abbreviations for *canceled*.

Cancer A sign of the Zodiac, *(the Crab)*; June 22–July 22.

Capricorn A sign of the Zodiac, *(the Goat)*; December 22–January 19.

carburetor

card-carrying   As an adjective.

carefree

Caribbean

carryout

CAT   Acronym for *computerized axial tomography* (e.g., *CAT scan*).

catalog or **catalogue**

cat-and-mouse

catbird seat

catch-22

cat-o'-nine-tails

catsup or **ketchup**

CATV   Acronym for *community antenna television*.

Caucasian

caveat emptor

CB or **citizens band**

cc   Abbreviation for *copy(copies) to* or *cubic centimeters*.

CDT   Acronym for *Central Daylight Time*.

C.E.   Abbreviation for *Common Era.*

cease-fire

-cede   Compound words ending in *-cede* are not usually hyphenated (e.g., *precede*).

-ceed   Compound words ending in *-ceed* are not usually hyphenated (e.g., *proceed*).

center   Capitalize only if part of a proper noun (e.g., *Rockefeller Center*).

Central America

CEO   Acronym for *chief executive officer.*

cert.   Abbreviation for *certificate, certification, certified, certify.*

cesarian section

cf.   Abbreviation for the Latin word *confer,* meaning "compare."

cg   Abbreviation for *centigram.*

chain-smoke

chaplain   Capitalize only if part of a title preceding a name (e.g., Chaplain Rogers).

chartreuse

check-   Compound words beginning with *check-* are not usually hyphenated (e.g., *checkbook*).

Cheyenne

chief   Capitalize only if part of a title preceding a name (e.g., Chief Oshkosh).

Chihuahua

chili con carne

chitchat

chutzpah

circadian

city   Capitalize only if part of a proper noun (e.g., *New York City*).

city-state

class-conscious

clean-cut   As an adjective.

clearheaded

clearinghouse

cliche or **cliché**

cliff-hanger

clique

cloak-and-dagger

close-   Compound words beginning with *close-* are not usually hyphenated (e.g., *closeout*); however, some are spelled as two words (e.g., *close call, close order, close quarters, close shave* and *close up*). When in doubt, consult a dictionary.

closed-captioned

closed-circuit   As an adjective.

closed-door

cm   Abbreviation for *centimeter.*

c/o   Abbreviation for *care of.*

co-   Compound words beginning with *co-* are not usually hyphenated (e.g., *cohabitation*). Exceptions are when the first letter following the previx is *o,* (e.g., *co-owner*) and when needed to avoid confusion (e.g., co-op).

coast   Capitalize only if referring to a major geographical region (e.g., *East Coast*).

coast guard   Capitalize only when referring to a specific one (e.g., *the United States Coast Guard*).

coast-to-coast

COBOL   Acronym for *common business-oriented language;* a computer programming language.

cobweb

COD or **C.O.D.**   Abbreviations for *cash on delivery.*

C. of C.   Abbreviation for *Chamber of Commerce.*

cold-blooded

coldhearted

colloq. Abbreviation for *colloquial* or *colloquialism*.

Colorado Abbreviation *CO*.

color-blind

coming-of-age As an adjective.

commander Capitalize only if part of a title preceding a name. (e.g., *Commander Murphy*).

common-law marriage

Common Market Also known as the *European Economic Community* (*EEC*).

commonwealth Capitalize only if part of a proper noun (e.g., *Commonwealth of Kentucky*).

communist Capitalize only if part of a proper noun (e.g., the Communist Party).

compact disc or **CD**

con. Abbreviation for the Latin word *contra*, meaning "against."

concierge

Connecticut Abbreviation *CT.*

connote To imply something beyond expressed meaning (e.g., *To some, the term* rest home *has negative connotations.* (Compare d*enote*.)

consumer price index Capitalize when referring to the United States index (*CPI*).

Continental Divide

continental shelf

Contra Capitalize when referring to the Nicaraguan rebel fighters.

contumacy Stubbornness (compare *contumely*).

contumely Haughty or insulting language (compare *contumacy*).

copr. Abbreviation for *copyright*.

copyediting

corps Capitalize only if part of a proper noun. (e.g., *Peace Corps*).

corpus delicti

cost-effective

counselor-at-law

coup de grâce

coup d'état

court-martial

CPA Acronym for *certified public accountant*.

CPR Acronym for *cardiopulmonary resuscitation*.

cross-   Compound words beginning with *cross-* are usually hyphenated (e.g., *cross-country*).

cu. ft.   Abbreviation for *cubic foot*.

cu. in.   Abbreviation for *cubic inch*.

cul-de-sac

cum laude   Latin term meaning *"with praise"*.

cuneiform

curriculum vitae or **CV**

customs   Capitalize only if part of a proper noun (e.g., *U.S. Customs Agency*).

cut-and-dried

cutthroat

cwt.   Abbreviation for.*hundredweight*.

d.   Abbreviation for deceased.

DA or **D.A.**   Abbreviation for *district attorney*.

dachshund

daylight saving time   Not *daylight savings time*.

d.b.a.   Abbreviation for *doing business as.*

DC   Acronym for *direct current.*

D day or D-day

DDT   Abbreviation for *dichlorodiphenyltrichloroethane;* an insecticide.

de-   Prefix meaning "down" or "away from". Hyphenate compound words beginning with *de-* when the first letter following the prefix is *e: de-emphasize.*

dead-   Compound words beginning with *dead-* are not usually hyphenated (e.g., *deadend*).

Dead Sea Scrolls

dean   Capitalize only if part of a formal title preceding a name (e.g., Dean McAllister).

decibel or dB

deep-   Compound words beginning with *deep-* are often hyphenated (e.g., *deep-dish*); however, some are spelled as two words (e.g., *deep freeze*) When in doubt, consult a dictionary.

-deep   Compound words ending in *-deep* are usually hyphenated (e.g., *skin-deep*).

def.   Abbreviation for *definition.*

déjà vu

Delaware   Abbreviation *DE.*

denote   To signify or indicate something (e.g., *The flag*

raised at half-mast denoted the death of someone in the town).
(Compare *connote*.)

denouement

dept. Abbreviation for *department*.

de rigueur

deriv. Abbreviation for *derivative*.

détente

deutschmark or DM Unit of German currency.

devil-may-care

di- Words beginning with *di-* are not usually hyphenated
(e.g., *diverse*).

dia- Words beginning with *dia-* are not usually hyphenated
(e.g., *diatribe*).

diag. Abbreviation for *diagonal*.

diam. Abbreviation for *diameter.*

dict. Abbreviation for *dictionary*.

dilettante

dir. Abbreviation for *director.*

dis- Words beginning with *dis-* are not usually hyphenated
(e.g., *disenchanted*).

diskette or floppy disk

dissertation   Abbreviation *diss.* (e.g., *doctoral diss.*).

dist.   Abbreviation for *district.*

District of Columbia   Abbreviation *D.C.*

DOA   Acronym for *dead on arrival.*

-doer   Compound words ending in *-doer* are not usually hyphenated (e.g., *wrongdoer*).

do-gooder

do-it-yourself

doomsday

do-or-die

door-to-door

Doppler effect

double-   Compound words beginning with *double-* are usually hyphenated (e.g., *double-check*).

double entendre

doublespeak

Dow-Jones average

down-   Compound words beginning with *down-* are not usually hyphenated (e.g., *downpour*).

-down   Compound words ending in *-down* are not usually hyphenated (e.g., *letdown*).

doz.   Abbreviation for *dozen.*

drachma   Unit of Greek currency.

dramatis personae   Latin term meaning "cast of characters."

drop-   Compound words beginning with *drop-* are not usually hyphenated (e.g., *dropout*) and are usually spelled out as two words (e.g., *drop cloth*).

druid or **Druid**

dry-   Compound words beginning with *dry-* are usually hyphenated (e.g., *dry-clean*).

due process

du jour   French term meaning "of the day."

dup.   Abbreviation for *duplicate.*

DWI or **DUI**   Acronyms for *driving while intoxicated* and *driving under the influence,* respectively.

dys-   Compound words beginning with *dys-* are not usually hyphenated (e.g., *dysfunction*).

E

ea.   Abbreviation for *each.*

earth   Capitalize only when referring to the planet.

east, eastern Capitalize when referring to a specific geographical location rather than a general direction (e.g., *Eastern Asia*).

eco-rich

ect- or **ecto-** Prefix meaning "outside" (e.g., *ectopic surgery*).

-ectomy Suffix meaning "surgical procedure" (e.g., *laryngectomy*).

edelweiss

EDT Acronym for *Eastern Daylight Time.*

EEG Acronym for *electroencephalogram* or *electronoencephalograph.*

égalité French word, meaning "equality."

EKG Abbreviation for *electrocardiogram* or *electrocardiograph.*

-elect Compound words ending in *-elect* are usually hyphenated (e.g., *governor-elect*).

electronic mail or **e-mail** The extensive computerized communication network (see entry in "Elements of Style A–Z").

electroshock therapy

emeritus; pl. **emeriti**

embassy Capitalize only if part of a proper noun (e.g., *the Chinese Embassy*).

embarrass

emigré   An individual who leaves her or his country for political reasons.

empty-handed

end-all   As a noun.

enfant terrible

endgame

endo-   Compound words beginning with *endo-* are not usually hyphenated (e.g., *endoskeletal*).

Eng.   Abbreviation for *England* or *English*.

engr.   Abbreviation for *engineer.*

en masse

entrée

entrepreneur

entomology   The study of insects (compare *etymology*).

EOF   Acronym for *end of file.*

EPA   Acronym for *Environmental Protection Agency.*

epi-   Compound words beginning with *epi-* are not usually hyphenated (e.g., *epicure*).

ERA   Acronym for *Equal Rights Amendment.*

equi- Compound words beginning with *equi-* are not usually hyphenated (e.g., *equidistant*).

ersatz

Eskimo, pl. **Eskimos**

ESP Acronym for *extrasensory perception*.

esp. Abbreviation for *especially*.

Esperanto

esprit de corps French term meaning "team spirit."

Esq. Abbreviation for *esquire;* a title that usually follows the names of lawyers, judges, justices of the peace, and other members of the legal profession.

EST Acronym for *Eastern Standard Time*.

est. Abbreviation for *established* and *estimated*.

et al. Abbreviation for the Latin term *et alia,* meaning "and others."

et cetera or ***etc.*** Latin term meaning "and so on."

et seq. Abbreviation for the Latin term *et sequentia,* meaning "and the following."

ETA Acronym for *estimated time of arrival*.

etymology The study of words and their origins (compare *entomology*).

Euclidean

Eurasian   An adjective used to describe an individual of European and Asian descent.

Eurodollar   A unit of European currency.

Evangelical or **evangelical**

evenhanded

ever-   Compound words beginning with *ever-* are not usually hyphenated (e.g., *evergreen, everlasting*), but are often hyphenated when modifying a noun (e.g., *ever-officious tyrant*).

ex-   Compound words beginning with *ex-* are not usually hyphenated (e.g., *excommunicate*); but are hyphenated when referring to an individual's former position (e.g., *ex-husband*).

exalt   To laud or praise (compare *exult*).

exc.   Abbreviation for *exception*.

Excalibur

excellency   Capitalize only if part of a title preceding a name (e.g., *His Excellency King Hussein*).

exceptionable   Intolerable or offensive (compare *exceptional*).

exceptional   Extraordinary (compare *exceptionable*).

excl.   Abbreviation for *excluded, exclusion*.

exec.   Abbreviation for *executive*.

exhibit   Capitalize only if referring to a specific exhibit (e.g., *The defense will now present to the jurors Exhibit A1*).

exhilarate

exodus   Capitalize only when referring to the second book of the Bible.

ex officio

exposé

ex post facto

extra-   Compound words beginning with *extra-* are not usually hyphenated (e.g., *extraneous*).

exult   To rejoice (compare *exalt*).

eye-   Compound words beginning with *eye-* are not usually hyphenated (e.g., *eyewitness*).

eye-catching

eye-opening

f., pl. ff.   Abbreviation for *and the following*.

F., Fah, Fahr.   Abbreviation for *Fahrenheit*.

FAA   Acronym for *Federal Aviation Administration*.

−faced Compound words ending in *-faced* are usually hyphenated (e.g., *open-faced*).

face-to-face As an adjective.

facsimile or **fax**

fail-safe

fair-weather

fait accompli French term, meaning "a deed or accomplishment that has already transpired."

far and away

faraway

Far East

fare-thee-well

farfetched

far-flung

farm- Compound words beginning with *farm-* are not usually hyphenated (e.g., *farmhand*).

faux pas French term, meaning "social blunder."

faze To disturb the composure of (compare *phase*).

FBI Acronym for *Federal Bureau of Investigation.*

FCC Acronym for *Federal Communications Commission.*

FDA Abbreviation for *Food and Drug Administration.*

federal Capitalize only if part of a proper noun (e.g., *Federal Communications Commission*).

federation Capitalize only if part of a proper noun (e.g., *Federation of African-American Physicians*).

fellow Capitalize only if part of a title preceding or following a name (e.g., *a Fellow of the History Department*).

fem. Abbreviation for *female* or *feminine.*

fiancé A man engaged to be married (compare *fiancée*).

fiancée A woman engaged to be married (compare *fiancé*).

-field Words ending in *-field* are not usually hyphenated (e.g., *battlefield*).

fifty-fifty

figurehead

figure of speech

filibuster

fin de siècle French term, meaning "end of the century."

finger- Compound words beginning with *finger-* are not usually hyphenated (e.g., *fingerprint*).

fire- Compound words beginning with *fire-* are not usually hyphenated (e.g., *firecracker*), and frequently are spelled out as two words (e.g., *fire truck*). When in doubt, consult a dictionary.

first- Compound words beginning with *first-* are not usually hyphenated (e.g., firsthand), and frequently are spelled out as two words (e.g., *first place*). When in doubt, consult a dictionary.

First World War or WWI

flagrante delicto Latin term meaning "in the act of committing a crime."

fleet Capitalize only if part of a proper noun (e.g., *Fleet Admiral Smith*).

fleur-de-lis

Florida Abbreviation *FL.*

Florida Keys

flotsam

-flower Compound words ending in *-flower* are not usually hyphenated (e.g., *cornflower*).

-fly Compound words ending in *-fly* are not usually hyphenated (e.g., *barfly*).

flyaway

fly-by-night As an adjective.

-fold Compound words ending in *-fold* are not usually hyphenated (e.g., *twofold*).

follow-up As a noun.

foot-and-mouth disease

foot-pound-second

foreclose

foregone conclusion

foreword   Introduction (compare *forward*).

forget-me-not

Formica   Trademarked name for a laminated product.

fortnight   Two weeks.

FORTRAN   Abbreviation for *formula translation;* a computer language.

forward   The direction (compare f*oreword*).

foundation   Capitalize only if part of a proper noun (e.g., *Make-a-Wish Foundation*).

4-H

four-letter word

Fourth of July or **Independence Day**

fr.   Abbreviation for *from.*

fracas, pl. fracases

franc   Unit of French currency.

free enterprise

free-for-all

French Compound words beginning with *French* are not usually hyphenated, and most often are spelled out as two words (e.g., *French horn*).

Freon Trademarked name for the aerosol propellant and refrigerant.

freq. Abbreviation for *frequency*.

Freudian slip To misspeak in a manner that reveals unconscious desires.

fricassee

Frisbee

f-stop

führer German word meaning "leader" or "tyrant."

-ful Compound words ending in *-ful* are not usually hyphenated (e.g., *purposeful*).

full- Compound words beginning with *full-* arc usually hyphenated (e.g., *full-bodied*).

full-time Sometimes abbreviated as *FT*.

fund-raising

f.v. Abbreviation for the Latin term *folio verso,* meaning "on the back of the page."

FYI Acronym for *for your information.*

G

g   Abbreviation for *gram*.

Galilean

galley proof

Gallup Poll

gamma ray

gangbusters

Garden of Eden

garden-variety

gauche

gee whiz

Geiger counter

Gemini   A sign of the Zodiac, (the Twins); May 21–June 21.

general practitioner or **GP**

genesis   Capitalize only when referring to the first book of the Bible.

geo-   Compound words beginning with *geo-* are not usually hyphenated (e.g., *geosphere*).

Georgia   Abbreviation *GA*.

German measles

gerrymander

Gestalt psychology

gesundheit

getaway   As a noun.

get-up-and-go   As a noun.

GI   Abbreviation for General Issue; refers to any member of the U.S. armed forces.

gl.   Abbreviation for *glossary*.

globe-trotter

Gnostic

go-between   As a noun.

go-getter

god   Capitalize only when using as a proper noun (e.g., *Thanks be to God*).

god-   Compound words beginning with *god-* are not usually hyphenated (e.g., *godfather*).

-goer   Compound words ending in *-goer* are not usually hyphenated (e.g., *concertgoer*).

goings-on

golden rule or **Golden Rule**

good-for-nothing   As a noun.

Good Friday

good-looking

Good Samaritan

Gordian knot

gospel   Capitalize only when referring to the books of Matthew, Mark, Luke and John in the Bible.

grade point average or **GPA**

grand-   Compound words beginning with *grand-* are not usually hyphenated (e.g., *granddaughter*).

grand mal seizure

grand prix, pl. **grand prix**

grant-in-aid   A type of public subsidy.

graph   Capitalize only if part of a proper noun (e.g., *Ericsonian Graph*).

gratis

grave accent

great-   Compound words beginning with *great-* are usually hyphenated (e.g., *great-aunt*).

Great Britain   England, Scotland, and Wales.

Great Depression

Great Lakes

Groundhog Day

Guam

guar. Abbreviation for *guarantee, guaranty.*

gubernatorial Referring to a governor.

guesswork

guideline

guild Capitalize only if part of a proper noun (e.g., *The Writers' Guild of America*).

gulf Capitalize only part of a proper noun (e.g., *Persian Gulf*).

gun- Compound words beginning with *gun-* are not usually hyphenated (e.g., *gunpowder*).

gung ho

gunnysack

gyroscope

ha-ha

habeas corpus

habitué French word, meaning "an individual who frequents the same place."

haiku, pl. **haiku**

Hail Mary

hair-trigger As an adjective.

half- Compound words beginning with *half-* are usually hyphenated (e.g., *half-baked*).

hallelujah

Halley's comet

hall of fame

hand over fist As an adverb.

Hanukkah or **Chanukkah**

hara-kiri Japanese term, meaning "ritual suicide."

Hare Krishna

harum-scarum

haut or *haute*   French term meaning "sophisticated."

Hawaii   Abbreviation *HI*.

H-bomb or **hydrogen bomb**

head-   Compound words beginning with *head-* are not usually hyphenated (e.g., *headdress*).

-headed   Compound words ending in *-headed* are not usually hyphenated (e.g., *thickheaded*).

headquarters   Capitalize only if part of a proper noun (e.g., *U.S. Marine Headquarters*). Abbreviations: *hdqrs., HQ.*

health maintenance organization or **HMO**

heart-   Compound words beginning with *heart-* are not usually hyphenated (e.g., *heartbreaker*).

-hearted   Compound words ending in *-hearted* are not usually hyphenated (e.g., *hardhearted*).

heavy-duty

Heimlich maneuver

helter-skelter

hem-   Compound words beginning with *hem-* are not usually hyphenated (e.g., *hematoma*).

herculean task

here-   Compound words beginning with *here-* are not usually hyphenated (e.g., *hereafter*).

here and now

herky-jerky

hex- Compound words beginning with *hex-* are not usually hyphenated (e.g., *hexagon*).

hi-fi or **high fidelity**

high- Compound words beginning with *high-* are usually hyphenated (e.g., *high-minded*), but not always (e.g., *high roller*). When in doubt, consult a dictionary.

High Church

High Court or **Supreme Court**

high school Capitalize only if part of a proper noun.

high-tech As an adjective.

high tech As a noun.

highway Capitalize only if part of a proper noun. Abbreviation: *hwy.*

hijinks or **high jinks**

Hindi The official language of India.

Hindu The people of India.

Hippocratic oath

Hispanic

hist. Abbreviation for *history, historical.*

hit-and-run

hitchhiker

hit-or-miss

HIV   Abbreviation for *human immunodeficiency virus.*

Hodgkin's disease

hoi polloi   Greek term meaning "the general population."

holo-   Compound words beginning with *hol-* or *holo-* are not usually hyphenated (e.g., *hologram*).

hole in one

hole-in-the-wall

Holy Ghost

Holy Spirit

home-   Compound words beginning with *home-* are not usually hyphenated (e.g., *homebred*).

homo-   Compound words beginning with *homo-* are not usually hyphenated (e.g., *homophone*).

Homo sapiens

honorable   Capitalize only if part of a title preceding a name (e.g., *the Honorable Susan White*). Abbreviation: *Hon.*

hook, line, and sinker

Hoosier

hootenanny

hors d'oeuvre

horse-and-buggy   As an adjective.

hospital   Capitalize only if part of a proper noun (e.g., *St. Elizabeth Hospital*). Abbreviation: *hosp.*

houndstooth or **hound's tooth**

house-   Compound words beginning with *house-* are not usually hyphenated (e.g., *housewarming*); however, many are spelled out as two words (e.g., *house call*). When in doubt, consult a dictionary.

-house   Compound words ending in *-house* are not usually hyphenated (e.g., *hothouse*).

house-to-house   As an adjective.

hr. or **h.**   Abbreviation for *hour.*

hubris

hue and cry

hullabaloo

Humpty-Dumpty

hung jury

hunt-and-peck

hush-hush

hydr- Compound words beginning with *hydr-* are not usually hyphenated (e.g., *hydraulics*).

hyper- Compound words beginning with *hyper-* are not usually hyphenated (e.g., *hypersound*).

hypo- Compound words beginning with *hypo-* are not usually hyphenated (e.g., *hypoallergenic*).

hyster- Compound words beginning with *hyster-* are not usually hyphenated (e.g., *hysterics*).

I

ibid or *ib.* Abbreviations for the Latin word *ibidem,* meaning "in the same place."

ice- Compound words beginning with *ice-* are often hyphenated (e.g., *ice-cold*); however, many are not hyphenated (e.g., *icebreaker*), and some are spelled out as two words (e.g., *ice pick*). When in doubt, consult a dictionary.

Ice Age or **ice age**

id. or *idem* Latin word meaning "the same."

Idaho Abbreviation *ID*.

i.e. Abbreviation for Latin term *id est,* meaning "that is."

ill- Compound words beginning with *ill-* are usually hyphenated (e.g., *ill-fated*).

ill at ease

Illinois Abbreviation *IL*.

illus. Abbreviation for *illustrated*.

Immaculate Conception

impasse

Impressionist or **impressionist**

impuissant French word meaning "without power."

in- Compound words beginning with *in-* are not usually hyphenated (e.g., *inorganic*).

-in Compound words ending in *-in* are usually hyphenated (e.g., *run-in*).

Inc. Abbreviation for *incorporated*. When part of a proper noun, a comma precedes it (e.g., *Integrated Systems, Inc.*).

incommunicado

index; pl. **indexes** or **indices**

Indian

Indiana Abbreviation *IN*.

Indo-European

infin. Abbreviation for *infinitive*.

in lieu of Instead of.

-in-law   Compound words ending in *-in-law* should be pluralized in the first word only (e.g., *sons-in-law*).

inner-city   As an adjective.

in re or **re**   Regarding.

ins and outs

inside out

inside track

insofar

inspector general   Capitalize only if part of a formal title preceding a name (e.g., *Inspector General Hadley*).

institute   Capitalize only if part of a proper noun (e.g., *The Hasting Institute*).

intelligentsia   The knowledgeable elite.

inter-   Compound words beginning with *inter-* are not usually hyphenated (e.g., *interdependent*); however, those containing a proper noun usually are (e.g., *inter-English*).

interj.   Abbreviation for *interjection*.

international date line

International Scientific Vocabulary or **ISV**

Internet or **internet**

Interpol Acronym for *International Criminal Police Organization*.

interstate Capitalize only if part of a proper noun (e.g., *U.S. Interstate Highway 101*).

int'l. Abbreviation for *international*.

in toto Entirely.

intra- Compound words beginning with *intra-* are not usually hyphenated (e.g., *intraregional*); however, if the second word begins with an *a*, they generally are (e.g., *intraregional; intra-active*).

intro- Compound words beginning with *intro-* are not usually hyphenated (e.g., *introduce*).

I/O Abbreviation for *input/output*.

IOU Acronym for *I owe you*.

Iowa Abbreviation *IA*.

ipso facto Latin term, meaning "by the nature of something."

IQ Acronym for *intelligence quotient*.

Iron Curtain or **iron curtain**

IRS Acronym for *Internal Revenue Service*.

iso- Compound words beginning with *iso-* are not usually hyphenated (e.g., *isometric*).

itin. Abbreviation for *itinerary*.

IV Acronym for *intravenous*.

Ivy League

J

Jack Frost

jack-in-the-box

jack-o'-lantern

jai alai

jam-pack

japan black

Japan wax

Jehovah's witness

jejune

Jekyll and Hyde

Jell-O Trademarked name for flavored gelatin.

jersey cow

jetsam

Jew A believer in Judaism and/or a descendent of the Hebrew people.

jib To cause to sail; to dodge (compare *jibe*).

jibe To agree or coincide (compare *jib*).

job-hop

joie de vivre French term, meaning "joy of living."

judge Capitalize only if part of a formal title preceding a name (e.g., *Judge Harold Wallace*).

Judgment Day

jujitsu or **jujutsu**

June bug or **june bug**

junta

junketeer

jurisprudence

jury-rig

justice of the peace Capitalize only if part of a formal title preceding a name (e.g., *Justice of the Peace Blair Campbell*).

kabob or **kebab** or **kebob**

kaleidoscope

Kansas   Abbreviation *KS.*

kayo or **KO**; pl. **kayoed** or **KO'd**

-keeper, -keeping   Compound words ending in -*keeper* or -*keeping* are not usually hyphenated (e.g., *housekeeper; bookkeeping*).

Kelvin scale

Kentucky   Abbreviation *KY.*

keystroke

key word

KGB   The Russian government's intelligence agency.

killjoy

kilogram or **kg**

kilohertz or **kHz**

kilometer or **km**

king   Capitalize only if part of a formal title preceding a name (e.g., *King George*).

kingdom come   The next world.

kitty-corner

Kleenex   Trademarked name for tissues.

kleptomaniac

klieg lights

knave   Forms of this word include *knavish; knavery.*

knickerbocker

knickknack

knock-down-drag-out

knock-kneed

know-how

know-it-all

knowledgeable

know-nothing

Know-Nothing   Capitalize when referring to the turn-of-the-century U.S. political organization that shunned Roman Catholics and other immigrants.

koala

Koran or **Qur'an**   The sacred scripture of Islam.

kosher

K ration

Ku Klux Klan or **KKK**   White supremacist organization.

kudos   Public honor.

kumquat

kvetch   Yiddish word, meaning "to complain."

KWIC   Abbreviation for *key word in context*.

kyrie   A prayer beginning with the words *Lord, have mercy*.

L

l., or **ll.**   Abbreviations for *line and lines,* respectively.

laboratory   Capitalize only if part of a proper noun (e.g., *Bell Laboratories*).

Labor Day

labor-intensive

Laetrile or **laetrile**   A drug used to treat cancer.

laid-back

laissez-faire

lake   Capitalize only if part of a proper noun (e.g., *Lake Titicaca*).

lambast or **lambaste**

lame-duck   As an adjective.

lame duck   As a noun.

LAN   Acronym for *local area network*.

land-   Compound words beginning with *land-* are not usually hyphenated (e.g., *landfill*).

-land   Compound words ending in *-land* are not usually hyphenated (e.g., *heartland*).

lane   Capitalize only if part of a proper noun (e.g., *Primrose Lane*). Abbreviations: *La.; Ln.*

lares and penates   Household objects.

largehearted

large-minded

largess or **largesse**

larva; pl. **larvae** or **larvas**

larynx; pl. **larynxes** or **larynges**

last hurrah

Last Supper

Lat. or **L.**   Abbreviations for *Latin*.

latecomer

latchkey

Latin American

Latter-day Saint or **Mormon**

layaway

lb or **lb.**   Abbreviation for *pound*.

LCD   Acronym for *liquid crystal display*.

lead-up   As a noun.

leadoff

league   Capitalize only if part of a proper noun (e.g., *National League*).

leap year

learn; past tense **learned**

leaseholder

least common denominator

LED   Acronym for *light-emitting diode*.

leeward

leeway

legatee   Individual named in a will (compare *legator*).

legator   Individual who authors a will (compare *legatee*).

Legionnaire's disease

legwork

leitmotif or **leitmotiv**   In art, a dominant theme or hallmark.

lend-lease

Leo   A sign of the Zodiac (the Lion); July 23–August 22.

leprechaun

-less   Compound words ending in *-less* are not usually hyphenated unless the last letter preceding the suffix is *l* (e.g., *joyless; mogul-less*).

lessee   Individual renting a property (compare *lessor*).

lessor   Individual renting out a property (compare *lessee*).

leuk-   Compound words beginning with *leuk-* are not usually hyphenated (e.g., *leukocyte*).

Levi's   Trademarked name for denim jeans.

lexicon; pl. **lexicons** or **lexica**

LF   Acronym for *low frequency*.

lg.   Abbreviation for *large*.

lib.   Abbreviation for *library*.

libel   Printed defamatory declaration (compare *slander*).

Liberty Bell

Libra   A sign of the zodiac (the Scales); September 23–October 23.

Library of Congress   Abbreviation *LOC*.

lic. Abbreviation for *license*.

lickety-split

lien A legal hold of personal property for its value against debt.

lieutenant Capitalize only when part of a formal title preceding a name. (*Lieutenant Briggs*). Abbreviations: *lieut., lt.*

life- Compound words beginning with *life-* are not usually hyphenated (e.g., *lifetime*).

life-and-death or **life-or-death**

Life Savers Trademarked name for roll candy.

lifestyle

-light Compound words ending in *-light* are not usually hyphenated (e.g., *flashlight*).

light-year

-like Compound words ending in *-like* are not usually hyphenated unless the first word ends in *l* (e.g., *firelike; mammal-like*).

lilliputian or **Lilliputian**

lily-livered

lily of the valley

lily-white

limited-access highway

-line Compound words ending in *-line* are not usually hyphenated (e.g., *sideline*).

Linotype

lionhearted

lion's share

lip-read

lip-synch or **lip-sync**

liq. Abbreviation for *liquid.*

lit. Abbreviation for *literature.*

liter or **litre** Abbreviations: *L, l, lit.*

literati The educated elite.

little- Compound words beginning with *little-* are hyphenated before a noun but spelled out as two words if they fall after a noun (e.g., *the little-known village; the village is little known*).

livable or **liveable**

lo and behold

-load Compound words ending in *-load* are not usually hyphenated (e.g., *download*).

loc. Abbreviation for *location.*

loc. cit. Abbreviation for the Latim term *loco citato*, meaning for "in the place cited."

lock, stock, and barrel   Entirely.

locum tenens; pl. *locum tenentes*   Latin term meaning "temporary substitute."

log on   As a verb.

log-on   As a noun.

long-drawn-out

lookout

look-see   As a noun.

loophole

loq.   Abbreviation for the Latin word *loquitur,* meaning "she or he speaks."

Lord's Prayer

Lou Gehrig's disease

Louisiana   Abbreviation *LA.*

lowercase

lowest common denominator

LSD   Acronym for *lysergic acid diethylamide,* a psychedelic drug.

ltd.   Abbreviation for *limited.*

lubricious   Lecherous (compare *lugubrious*).

lugubrious   Mournful (compare *lubricious*).

luster or **lustre**

macabre

Mace   Trademarked name a for chemical compound commercially sold as an anti-assailant weapon.

Machiavellian

machismo

Mach number

macr- or **macro-**   Compound words beginning with *macro-* are not usually hyphenated (e.g., *macrofossil*).

made-to-order   As an adjective.

made-up   As an adjective.

madras

maelstrom

magna cum laude   Latin term meaning *"with great praise."*

maharaja or **maharajah**   Hindi word meaning "a prince whose caste ranking is above a raja."

Maine   Abbreviation *ME*.

maize

make-believe

makeup   As a noun.

make up   As a verb.

malaise

malleable

manageable

-mania   Compound words ending in *-mania* are not usually hyphenated (e.g., *egomania*).

Manitoba   Canadian province; abbreviation *MB*.

manuf.   Abbreviation for *manufacturing*, *manufacture*.

Mardi Gras   French term meaning "Fat Tuesday."

marijuana

Maryland   Abbreviation *MD*.

Massachusetts   Abbreviation *MA*.

matchmaker

master key

M.D.   Abbreviation for *medical doctor*.

medieval

mediocre

meiosis

ménage à trois

menorah A Jewish candelabrum with nine candles used to celebrate Hanukkah, the Festival of Lights.

menswear

merry-go-round

meta- or **met-** Compound words beginning with *meta-* or *met-* are not usually hyphenated (e.g., *metaphase; metaphysical; metamorphosis*).

mezzanine

mfd. Abbreviation for *manufactured.*

Michigan Abbreviation *MI.*

micro- Compound words beginning with *micro-* are not usually hyphenated (e.g., *microbrewery; microcosm*).

mid- Compound words beginning with *mid-* are not usually hyphenated (i.e., *midtown; midday; midpoint*). When in doubt, consult a dictionary.

middle class As a noun.

middle-class As an adjective.

middleman

midlife

Midwest   Common abbreviated version of the term *Middle West*, indicating the North Central region of the United States.

MiG   A type of fighter plane (e.g., *MiG-19*).

milli-   Prefix which denotes one-thousandth of a unit.

mimosa

mini-   Compound words beginning with *mini-* are not usually hyphenated (e.g., *miniskirt; minivan; miniseries*).

Minnesota   Abbreviation *MN*.

mint julep

mis-   Compound words beginning with *mis-* are usually not hyphenated (e.g,. *misanthrope; misfit; mistrial; misunderstand*).

Miss   Traditional title of an unmarried woman (e.g., *Miss Santiago*).

Mississippi   Abbreviation *MS*.

Missouri   Abbreviation *MO*.

mix up   As a verb.

mix-up   As a noun.

Molotov cocktail   A hand grenade that can be homemade with gasoline, a bottle, and a piece of cloth as the wick.

-monger Compound words ending in *-monger* are not hyphenated (e.g., *fishmonger; warmonger*).

mono- Compounds beginning with *mono-* are not usually hyphenated (e.g., *monosyllabic; monochrome*).

monsignor

Montana Abbreviation *MT.*

Monterey Jack

mosaic

-mouthed Compound words ending in *-mouthed* are not usually hyphenated (e.g., *bigmouthed; widemouthed*).

mouth-to-mouth

moveable or **movable**

mozzarella

mpg Abbreviation for *miles per gallon.*

mph Abbreviation for *miles per hour.*

Mr. Abbreviation for the title *mister,* indicating a man of indeterminate marital status (e.g., *Mr. McFadden*).

Mrs. Abbreviation for the title *mistress,* indicating a married woman (e.g., *Mrs. LaRouge*).

Ms. Generic abbreviated title, indicating a woman of indeterminate marital status (e.g., *Ms. Jones*).

multi-   Compound words beginning with multi- are not usually hyphenated (e.g., *multimillionaire*).

muumuu

Muzak

MVP   Acronym for *most valuable player*.

myrrh

NAACP   Acronym for *National Association for the Advancement of Colored People*.

naïve or naive

name-calling

name-dropping

nano-   Prefix which denotes one-billionth of a unit.

narcissism

narcotic

narrow-minded

NASA   Acronym for *National Aeronautics and Space Administration*.

nationwide

NATO   Acronym for *North Atlantic Treaty Organization.*

nausea   Forms of this word include *nauseating; nauseous; nauseated.*

naval   Of or pertaining to the Navy

navel   A mammal's bellybutton.

navigable

navy blue

N.B.   Abbreviation for the Latin term *nota bene,* meaning "mark well."

NBA   Acronym for *National Basketball Association.*

nearsighted

Nebraska   Abbreviation *NE.*

neck and neck

ne'er-do-well

neg.   Abbreviation for *negative.*

negligee

neo-   Compound words beginning with *neo-* are not usually hyphenated (e.g., *neophyte*); however, there are exceptions. Consult a dictionary; if a word is not listed, use a hyphen (e.g., *neo-impressionism*).

nest egg

netherworld

Neufchâtel

nevertheless

newborn

New Brunswick   Canadian province; abbreviation *NB*.

newfangled

new-fashioned

newfound

Newfoundland   Canadian province; abbreviation *NF*.

New Hampshire   Abbreviation *NH*.

New Jersey   Abbreviation *NJ*.

newlywed

New Mexico   Abbreviation *NM*.

news-   Compound words beginning with *news-* are not usually hyphenated (e.g., *newsstand*).

New York   Abbreviation *NY*.

night-   Compound words beginning with *night-* are not usually hyphenated (e.g., *nightclub; nighttime; nightgown; nightlife*).

nil   Meaning "nothing" or "zero."

n.m. or **n.mi.**   Abbreviations for *nautical mile*.

no. or **nos.**   Abbreviations for *number* and *numbers*, respectively

nobody

no-holds-barred

no one

non-   Words beginning with *non-* are not usually hyphenated (e.g., *nonaligned; nonrestrictive; noncontroversial*).

nonprofit

non seq.   Abbreviation for the Latin term, *non sequitur*, meaning "it does not follow."

noontime

no place

North Carolina   Abbrevation *NC.*

North Dakota   Abbreviation *ND.*

north-northeast

north-northwest

note-   Compound words beginning with *note-* are not usually hyphenated (e.g., *noteworthy*).

nouveau riche   French term meaning "newly rich." Plural: *nouveaux riches*.

Nova Scotia Canadian province; abbreviation *NS*.

nowadays

noway or **noways**

nowhere

no-win As an adjective.

nth degree

nucle- or **nucleo-** Compound words beginning with *nucle-* or *nucleo-* are not usually hyphenated (e.g., *nucleotide*).

null and void

nunchaka A Japanese weapon.

Northwest Territories Canadian province; abbreviation *NT*.

OB-GYN Acronym for *obstetrician-gynecologist* or *obstetrics-gynecology*.

objet d'art French term meaning "article valued for its artistic nature."

observatory

obsessive-compulsive

occ. Abbreviation for *occasional*, *occasionally*.

occur Forms of this word include *occurred; occurring; occurrence*.

ocean- Compound words beginning with *ocean-* are not usually hyphenated (e.g., *oceangoing*).

off- or **-off** For compound words beginning with *off-* or ending in *-off*, follow the guidance of a dictionary, as hyphenation is variable (e.g., *off-peak* or *offsides; stop-off* or *liftoff*). If the word not listed, hyphenate it.

ogle

ogre

Ohio Abbreviation *OH*.

okay or **OK**; pl. **OKs** or **okays**

Oklahoma Abbreviation *OK*.

omni- Compound words beginning with *omni-* are not usually hyphenated (e.g., *omnipotent; omnivorous; omnibus*).

one- When used as part of a fraction, *one-* should be hyphenated (e.g., *one-half; one-ninth*). When used as a prefix, *one-* should also be hyphenated (e.g., *one-sided* opinion; *one-time* star; *one-person* job) .

ongoing

onionskin

Ontario Canadian province; abbreviation *ON*.

onward or **onwards**

op. cit.   Abbreviation for the Latin phrase *opere citato,* meaning "in the work cited."

opossum

Oregon   Abbreviation *OR.*

origami

oste- or **osteo-**   Compound words beginning with *oste-* or *osteo-* are not usually hyphenated (e.g., *osteoclast; osteophyte*).

out- or **-out**   For compound words beginning with *out-* or ending in *-out,* follow the guidance of a dictionary, as hyphenation is variable (e.g., *out-of-date* or *outdated*). If the word is not listed, hyphenate it.

ovenbaked

over- or **-over**   A hyphen is not usually used when *over-* is a prefix (e.g., *overrate; overlook; overwhelm*). As a suffix, *-over* is particularly variable (e.g., *stopover;carry-over*). Consult a dictionary when using *over* as a suffix or a prefix. If the word is not listed, hyphenate it.

oyez   A command used by court and public officials to effect silence.

oz.   Abbreviation for *ounce* or *ounces.*

p & h Abbreviation for *postage and handling*.

PAC Acronym for *political action committee*.

painkiller

painstaking

pan- Most compound words beginning with *pan-* are not hyphenated (e.g., *panhandle; panfry; pancake*); however, compounds combined with a proper noun are hyphenated (e.g., *pan-European*).

pantsuit

parallel Forms of this word include *paralleling; paralleled; parallels*.

parentheses

parishioner

parliamentary

part of speech

part-time Sometimes abbreviated as *PT*.

PASCAL or **Pascal** A computer programming language; named for Blaise Pascal.

passers-by

pasteurize

pastiche A literary, musical or artistic work that imitates or borrows from previous works. Derived from the Italian word *pasticcio*.

pastor Capitalize only if part of a formal title preceding a name (*Pastor Quinn*).

pastrami or **pastromi** A Yiddish word for a type of popular smoked beef.

patchouli or **patchouly** An East Indian variety of shrubby mint that yields a fragrant essential oil.

pedal A foot lever, or to operate a foot lever (compare *peddle*).

peddle To sell (compare *pedal*).

penitentiary

Pennsylvania Abbreviation *PA*.

percent

perk A legal term describing fringe benefits; short for *perquisite*.

permissible

phase A period of change, or to make changes (compare *faze*).

picaresque Of or having to do with rogues.

piccolo

pick-me-up

pico-   Prefix which denotes one-trillionth of a unit.

picturesque

-piece   Compound words ending in *-piece* are not hyphenated (e.g., *showpiece*).

pigeon

piranha

pirouette

Pisces   A sign of the Zodiac *(the Fishes);* February 19–March 20.

pistachio

pistil   A part of a flower (compare *pistol*).

pistol   A type of weapon (compare *pistil*).

pj's   Abbreviated nickname for *pajamas.*

PLO   Acronym for *Palestine Liberation Organization.*

p.m. or **P.M.**   Abbreviation for the Latin term *post meridiem,* meaning "after noon."

poinsettia

point-blank

politicking

pom-pom or **pompon**   *Pom-pom* is sometimes used to mean an automatic weapon; *pompons* are puffy objects used primarily by cheerleaders and on clothing.

pore   To look at something intently, or a tiny opening in a membrane (compare *pour*).

post-   Compound words beginning with *post-* are not usually hyphenated (e.g., *postdoctoral*). If the word not listed in a dictionary, hyphenate it (e.g., *post-bellum*).

potatoes

pour   To dispense, or to rain hard (compare *pore*).

POW   Abbreviation for *prisoner of war*.

pre-   Most words beginning with *pre-* are not hyphenated unless the first letter following the prefix is *e* (e.g. *pre-empt; pre-exist*). Consult a dictionary; hyphenate the word if it is not listed.

premier   Another name for the prime minister of a government based on a council of ministers.

Prince Edward Island   Canadian province; abbreviation *PE*.

principal   Most important, or person in charge (compare *principle*).

principle   Idea, or code of conduct (compare *principal*).

prima facie   Latin term meaning "at first glance."

privilege

pro- As a prefix *pro-* is not usually hyphenated unless its meaning is literally "being for something" (e.g., *pro-peace*).

prophecy A prediction (compare *prophesy*).

prophesy To predict (compare *prophecy*).

psych- or **psycho-** Compound words beginning with *psych-* or *psycho-* are not usually hyphenated (e.g., *psychotherapy*).

Puerto Rico Abbreviation *PR*.

put down As a verb.

put-down As a noun.

Q & A Abbreviation for *question and answer*.

Q.E.D. Abbreviation of the Latin phrase *quod erat demonstrandum,* meaning "which was to be demonstrated."

qty. Abbreviation for *quantity*.

quadri, quadr-, quadru- Compound words beginning with these prefixes, meaning "fourfold," are not usually hyphenated (e.g., *quadrilateral; quadriceps; quadruple*).

qual. or **qlty**. Abbreviation for *quality*.

quandary

quarantine

quartet　Or quartette

quasi　This word, meaning "seemingly" in Latin, can be used as an ordinary adjective to modify a noun (e.g., *quasi god; quasi food*). When combined with an adjective or modifier, *quasi-* is hyphenated (e.g., *quasi-professional; quasi-judicial*).

quay　A docking area.

Quebec　Canadian province; abbreviation *PQ*.

queen-size

quesadilla　A Mexican grilled sandwich made with tortilla and cheese.

queue　To stand on line, or a line itself.

questionnaire

quick-　When using *quick-* as a prefix, consult a dictionary to verify hyphenation.

quicksand

quick-witted

quid　British slang for the pound, a form of currency.

quixotic

quot.　Abbreviation for *quotation*.

quota

R

rabbi   Capitalize only when part of a title preceding a name (e.g., *Rabbi Handelman*).

raccoon

racquet or **racket**   Either spelling is considered to be acceptable to mean the handled piece of equipment used for sports such as tennis or squash.

radar   Acronym for *radio detecting and ranging*, meaning the use of radio waves to detect an object.

radio-   Compound words beginning with *radio-* are generally not hyphenated (e.g., *radiosensitive; radioecology*). Consult a dictionary for exceptions (e.g., *radio wave*).

rain-   Compound words beginning with *rain-* are not usually hyphenated (e.g., *rainwater; raindrop; rainstorm; rainbow*). Consult a dictionary for exceptions to this rule (e.g., *rain check*).

raisin   A dried grape.

raison d'être   French term meaning *"reason for being."*

RAM   Acronym for *random access memory*.

ratatouille

R & B   Abbreviation for *rhythm and blues*.

re-   Compound words beginning with *re-* are not usually hyphenated. Two exceptions are: when using the hyphen to avoid confusion with another word (e.g., *re-sign*, meaning "to sign again", as opposed to *resign,* meaning "to quit"); and when using a hyphen to separate like letters (e.g., *re-elect; re-establish; re-energize*). Consult a dictionary if unsure, and use a hyphen if the word in question is not listed there.

recidivist   A criminal justice term meaning "repeat of-fender."

recipes

reconnaissance

recur   Forms of this word include *recurred; recurring; recurrence.*

recyclable

red-eye   An overnight flight.

redhead, redheaded, red-haired

referendum

reg.   Abbreviation for *regular.*

regime

REM   Acronym for *rapid eye movement;* which refers to patterns of sleep and dreaming.

remissible   Forgivable.

rerun

resistible

restaurateur

reservoir

retractable

retro- Compound words beginning with *retro-* are usually not hyphenated (e.g., *retroactive; retrolingual*).

Rev. Abbreviation for *Reverend.*

reveille The well-known bugle call at daybreak.

Rhode Island Abbreviation *RI.*

rhododendron

rhyme

rhythmic

right-of-way

rigor mortis

RIP Acronym for the Latin term *requiescat in pace,* meaning "rest in peace."

rip-off As a noun.

Rip off As a verb.

rip-roaring

role-play As a verb.

roll-on As an adjective or a noun.

ROM   Acronym for *read-only memory*.

roofs   The plural form of *roof*.

-room   Compound words ending in *-room* are not usually hyphenated (e.g. *bedroom; elbowroom; showroom*).

Rosh Hashanah or **Rosh Hashanah**   The Jewish New Year.

ROTC   Acronym for *Reserve Officers' Training Corps*.

rpm   Abbreviation for *revolutions per minute*.

RSVP   Acronym for the French term *répondez s'il vous plaît,* meaning "please reply."

rubella   Also known as *German measles*.

run-of-the-mill

S

s/a   Abbreviation for *subject to approval*.

Sabbath

sabbatical

saber or **sabre**

sabotage

saboteur

saccharin   An artificial sweetener (compare *saccharine*).

saccharine   Overly sweet; syrupy (compare *saccharin*).

sadomasochism

SASE   Acronym for *self-addressed stamped envelope*.

safeguard

safe house

Sagittarius   A sign of the Zodiac (the Archer); November 22–December 21.

Saint Bernard or **St. Bernard**

Saint Patrick's Day

St. Valentine's Day

sake or **saki**

SALT   Acronym for *Strategic Arms Limitation Treaty*.

salt-and-pepper   As an adjective.

saltpeter

salutary   Good, healing (compare *salutatory*).

salutatory   Hospitable (compare *salutary*).

Salvation Army

Samaritan

samurai

S and L or **S & L**   Abbreivations for *savings and loan.*

S & M or **S/M**   Abbreviations for *sadomasochism.*

sangfroid   French word meaning "self-possession."

Sanskrit

Santa Claus

SAT   Acronym for *Scholastic Aptitude Test.*

Saskatchewan   Canadian province; abbreviation *SK.*

Satan

saturnalia

savanna or **savannah**

savant

savoir faire   French term meaning "deftness in handling any situation with grace and tact."

say-so

schlemiel   Yiddish word meaning "chump."

schlep   Yiddish word meaning "to haul."

schmooze   Yiddish word meaning "to chat or mingle."

school   Capitalize only if part of a proper noun (*Richmond Elementary School*).

school- Compound words beginning with *school-* are not usually hyphenated (e.g., *schoolteacher*).

science fiction Abbreviations: *sci-fi; SF.*

scler- Compound words beginning with *scler-* are not usually hyphenated (e.g., *scleroderma*).

-scope Compound words ending in *-scope* are not usually hyphenated (e.g., *periscope*).

Scorpio A sign of the Zodiac, (the Scorpion); October 24–November 21.

screenplay

scripture Capitalize only when referring to the Bible.

s.d. Abbreviation for *same day.*

sea- Compound words beginning with *sea-* are not usually hyphenated (e.g., *seaboard*).

search warrant

seat-of-the-pants As an adjective.

sec. or s. Abbreviations for *second; secretary.*

secretary general Capitalize only if part of a title preceding a name (Secretary General Hammarskjold).

seder or Seder The Jewish Passover feast.

Seeing Eye dog Trademarked name for the guide dog for the blind.

seesaw

self- Compound words beginning with *self-* are usually hyphenated (e.g., *self-esteem*).

semi- Compound words beginning with *semi-* are not usually hyphenated (e.g., *semisoft*); however, some are (e.g., *semi-independent*). When in doubt, consult a dictionary.

Semitic

senator Capitalize only if part of a formal title preceding a name (e.g., *Senator Hayakawa*).

senior citizen

sensual Pleasurable to the body or sexual (compare *sensuous*).

sensuous Appealing to the senses (compare *sensual*).

seq. Abbreviation for *sequel, sequence,* or *sequitur* (Latin word, meaning "it follows").

Serbo-Croatian

sergeant-at-arms Capitalize only if part of a formal title preceding a name (e.g., *Sergeant-at-Arms Perkins*).

Sermon on the Mount

Seventh-day Adventist

Seven Wonders of the World

s/h Abbreviation for *shipping and handling*.

shalom   Hebrew word meaning "peace."

Shangri-la

sheikh or **sheik**

shell-shocked

shogun

short-   Compound words beginning with *short-* are not usually hyphenated (e.g., *shortchanged*).

shutterbug

shylock

sic   Latin word meaning "so" or "thus."

SIDS   Acronym for *Sudden Infant Death Syndrome.*

sierra

sight-seeing

sign-off   As a verb.

simpleminded

simulacrum; pl. **simulacra** or **simulacrums**

sine qua non   Latin term meaning "essential thing."

sitting duck

skullduggery or **skulduggery**

SL   Abbreviation for *sea level.*

slander   Spoken defamatory statement (compare *libel*).

slapdash

slice-of-life   As an adjective.

sm. or **sml.** or **S**, or **s**   Abbreviations for *small.*

small-claims court

smoke screen

SN   Abbreviation for *serial number.*

snafu   Acronym for *situation normal all fouled up.*

snow-   Compound words beginning with *snow-* are not usually hyphenated (e.g., *snowshoe*).

so-and-so

so-called

socialism, socialist   Capitalize only if referring to the political party or one of its members.

socio-   Compound words beginning with *socio-* are not usually hyphenated (e.g., *sociopolitical*).

some-   Compound words beginning with *some-* are not usually hyphenated (e.g., *sometimes*).

SOP   Acronym for *standard operating procedure.*

SOS Distress signal; acronym for *save our ship* or *save our souls*.

South Carolina Abbreviation *SC*.

South Dakota Abbreviation *SD*.

sp. Abbreviation for *spell, spelled* or *special*.

Spartan

SPF Acronym for *sun protection factor,* used in commercial sunscreens.

spiel

spur-of-the-moment As an adjective.

sq. yd. Abbreviation for *square yard*.

SRO Acronym for *standing room only* or *single-room occupancy*.

SS Acronym for *Social Security*.

SST Acronym for *supersonic transport*.

staff; pl. staff Personnel.

Staff; pl. staffs or **staves** A long stick or pole, or lines used in musical notation.

stand-in

standoff

Stars and Stripes

state   Capitalize only if referring to a specific state (e.g., *Washington State*).

state-of-the-art   As an adjective.

state of the art   As a noun.

station   Capitalize only if part of a proper noun (e.g., *Grand Central Station*).

Statue of Liberty

status quo

std.   Abbreviation for *standard*.

step-   Compound words beginning with *step-* are not usually hyphenated (e.g., *stepmother*).

stet   Latin word meaning "let it stand."

stick-in-the-mud

-storm   Compound words ending in *-storm* are not usually hyphenated (e.g., *hailstorm*).

straight As or **straight A's**

Sturm und Drang   German term meaning "the wear and tear of life."

Styrofoam   Trademarked name for polystyrene plastic.

subj.   Abbreviation for *subject*.

summa cum laude   Latin term meaning "with highest honor or praise."

super-   Compound words beginning with *super-* are not usually hyphenated (e.g., *supernova*).

supra-   Compound words beginning with *supra-* are not usually hyphenated (e.g., *supraliminal*).

supreme court   Capitalize only when part of a proper noun (e.g., *United States Supreme Court*).

sur-   Compound words beginning with *sur-* are not usually hyphenated (e.g., *surname*).

surface-to-air missile

surgeon general   Capitalize only if part of a formal title preceding a name (e.g., *Surgeon General Joycelyn Elders*).

s.v.   Abbreviation for the Latin term *sub verso,* meaning "below the word."

Swahili

SWAK   Acronym for *sealed with a kiss.*

swan song

swastika

SWAT   Acronym for *special weapons and tactics.*

syllabus; pl. **syllabi** or **syllabuses**

syn-, sym-   Compound words beginning with *syn-* or *sym-* are not usually hyphenated (e.g., *synergy; symphonic*).

syn.   Abbreviation for *synonym, synonymous.*

synagogue or **synagog**

synch or **sync**

synd. Abbreviation for *syndicate*.

sys. or **syst.** Abbreviations for *system*.

t. or **tn.** Abbreviations for *ton*.

tableau; pl. **tableaux** or **tableaus**

tabula rasa Latin term meaning "blank mind" or "clean slate."

tae kwon do or **Tae Kwon Do**

take-in As a noun.

take in As a verb.

takeout As a noun or an adjective.

take out As a verb.

tallyho

Talmud

Taurus A sign of the Zodiac, (the Bull), April 20–May 20.

taxpayer

tax shelter

Tay-Sachs disease

TB   Acronym for *tuberculosis*.

TBA   Acronym for *to be announced*.

tbsp. or **T.**, or **tb.**   Abbreviations for *tablespoon, table-spoonful*.

teacher's pet

teamster   Capitalize only when referring to the Teamsters Union or its members.

tech.   Abbreviation for *technical* or *technology*.

TKO   Acronym for *technical knockout*.

Technicolor   Trademarked name for a film coloring process.

teetotaller or **teetotaler**

Teflon   Trademarked name for a nonstick surface coating on cookware.

tel-   Compound words beginning with *tel-* are not usually hyphenated (e.g., *telephone*).

temp.   Abbreviation for *temporary*.

ten-cent store

Ten Commandments

tender loving care or **TLC**

Tennessee   Abbreviation *TN*.

term. or **trm.**   Abbreviations for *terminal* or *terminate*.

terra-cotta

terra firma

territory   Capitalize only if part of a proper noun. (e.g., *Yukon Territory*).

tête-à-tête   French term meaning "private one-to-one meeting."

Texas   Abbreviation *TX*.

T formation

TGIF   Acronym for *thank God it's Friday*.

Thanksgiving Day

theo-   Compound words beginning with *theo-* are not usually hyphenated (e.g., *theologian*).

theater

there-   Compound words beginning with *there-* are not usually hyphenated (e.g., *thereabouts*).

therm-   Compound words beginning with *therm-* are not usually hyphenated (e.g., *thermometer*).

thief; pl. **thieves**

think tank

third world or **Third World**

3-D or **three-dimensional**

threesome

throughway or **thruway**   Capitalize only if part of a proper noun (e.g., *the New York Thruway*).

thumbnail

thyr-   Compound words beginning with *thyr-* are not usually hyphenated (e.g., *thyroid*).

tiebreaker

time-   Compound words beginning with *time-* are not usually hyphenated (e.g., *timesaver*), and are frequently spelled out as two words (*time travel*). When in doubt, consult a dictionary.

TNT   Acronym for *trinitrotoluene,* an explosive.

-to-be

to-and-fro

tongue-tied

tongue-twister

tonight

tool-   Compound words beginning with *tool-* are not usually hyphenated (e.g., *toolbox*).

topflight   As an adjective.

top flight   As a noun.

Top 40

Torah

tour de force   French term meaning "great feat."

to wit   Namely

township   Capitalize only if part of a proper noun (e.g., *Dakota Township*).

townspeople

trademark or **TM**

trans-   Compound words beginning with *trans-* are not usually hyphenated (e.g., *transcendental*).

trans. or **tr.**   Abbreviations for *transfer.*

treasury   Capitalize only if part of a proper noun (e.g., *United States Treasury*).

treaty   Capitalize only if part of a proper noun (e.g., *Treaty of Versailles*).

tri-   Compound words beginning with *tri-* are not usually hyphenated (e.g., *tricolored*).

trompe l'oeil   French term meaning "to fool the eye"; usually refers to the style of painting.

trop- Compound words beginning with *trop-* are not usually hyphenated (e.g., *tropography*).

troubadour

troubleshoot

trousseau; pl. **trousseaux** or **trousseaus**

truant officer

true-blue

true-life As an adjective.

truelove

trump card

trumped-up

tsetse fly

T-shirt or **tee shirt**

tsp. or **t.,** or **tspn.** Abbreviations for *teaspoon.*

T square

Tudor house

Turkish bath

turncoat

turning point

turnpike Capitalize only if part of a proper noun (e.g., *New Jersey Turnpike*).

turnstile

tutti-frutti

TV

twelve-step program

twice-told

two-by-four

two-ply

two-time

two-way street

tying or **tieing**

typo Abbreviation for *typographical error.*

U

U A Burmese term used as a title to designate honor.

u.c. Abbreviation for *upper case.*

UHF   Acronym for *ultrahigh frequency*.

ukulele or **ukelele**

ultimo   Latin word meaning "in the prior month."

ultra-   Compound words beginning with *ultra-* are not usually hyphenated (e.g., *ultramodern*); however, some are (e.g., *ultra-acidic*). When in doubt, consult a dictionary.

umlaut   A diacritical marking (··)sometimes used in writing vowels.

un-   Compound words beginning with *un-* are not usually hyphenated (e.g., *unnecessary*); however, some are: (e.g., *un-American*). When in doubt, consult a dictionary.

unaware   As an adjective.

unawares   As an adverb.

unbeliever

uncalled-for

under-   Compound words beginning with *under-* are not usually hyphenated (e.g., *underdog*); however, some are (e.g., *under way*). When in doubt, consult a dictionary.

under-the-counter   As an adjective.

under-the-table   As an adjective.

undersize or **undersized**

unheard of

unisex

unkn. or **unk.**   Abbreviations for *unknown*.

Unknown Soldier

up-   Compound words beginning with *up-* are not usually hyphenated (e.g., *update*). For rules on nouns and adjectives made using *-up* as a suffix, consult a dictionary, as these compounds are variable (e.g., *makeup, pileup; runner-up, cover-up*).

up-and-coming

uppercase

up-to-date   As an adjective.

up-to-the-minute

upward   Not *upwards*.

USDA   Acronym for *United States Department of Agriculture*.

useable or **usable**

user-friendly

USPS   Acronym for *United States Postal Service*.

Utah   Abbreviation *UT*.

util.   Abbreviation for *utility*.

U-turn

V

V   Abbreviation for *voltage, volts.*

v. or **vb.**   Abbreviations for *verb* or *verbs.*

VA   Acronym for *Veterans Administration.*

vacuum

val.   Abbreviation for *value, valued.*

valet parking

vanilla

vantage point

var.   Abbreviation for *variable, variant, various, variety.*

VAT   Acronym for *value-added tax;* a United Kingdom tax that foreigners can get refunded depending on the amount of tax that they have paid during their travels.

VCR   Acronym for *videocassette recorder.*

veg.   Abbreviation for *veggies, vegetable.*

vena cava

venereal disease   Abbreviation *VD.*

venetian blinds

venue   A term meaning "place"; derived from the French.

Venus's-flytrap

ver.   Abbreviation for *version*. The plural *vss.* is the abbreviated form of *versions*.

verbatim

verdant   Green or greenish.

vermilion or **vermillion**   A bright red color.

Vermont   Abbreviation *VT.*

vermouth

versus   Abbreviated as *vs.* for common usage (e.g., *Burly vs. Wrestlemonger*) and *v.* in reference to legal matters (e.g., *Roe v. Wade*).

vert.   Abbreviation for *vertical*.

vertebrae

vested interest

veto   Forms of this word include *vetoes; vetoing; vetoed.*

VHF   Acronym for *very high frequency.*

VHS   Acronym for *video home system.*

v.i.   Abbreviation for the Latin term *vide infra*, meaning "see below."

vice-   Compound words beginning with *vice-* are generally spelled as two separate words (e.g., *vice president; vice principal*). Consult a dictionary for exceptions to this rule.

vice versa

vichyssoise   A type of French soup.

videodisc

video game

videotape

vie   Forms of this word include *vied; vying.*

Vietnam

vincible   Conquerable; the antonym is invincible.

VIP   Acronym for *very important person.*

virescent   Having a green or greenish color.

Virginia   Abbreviation *VA.*

Virgin Islands   Abbreviation *VI.*

Virgo   A sign of the Zodiac, (the Virgin); August 23 – September 22.

virtual reality

vis-à-vis   French term meaning "face to face."

vis.   Abbreviation for *visual.*

vital signs

vitamin The letters designating specific vitamins should be capitalized (e.g., *vitamin B; vitamin B-12; vitamin K; B complex; D*).

viva voce Latin term meaning "by word of mouth."

vivify To give life or new life to something.

viz. Abbreviation for the Latin term *videlicet*, meaning "namely."

V neck As a noun.

V-necked As an adjective.

vocab. Abbreviation for *vocabulary*.

voice-over

voilà French word meaning "here it is" or "here is."

vol. Abbreviation for *volume*.

volatile

volleyball

voluble Talkative.

voodoo

vox populi Latin term meaning "the voice of the people."

v.s. Abbreviation of the Latin term *vide supra*, meaning "see above."

W

w.   Abbreviation for *water, watt, width,* or *with.*

waive

walkout   As a noun.

walk out   As a verb.

wallflower

Wall Street

want ad

war   Capitalize only if part of a proper noun (e.g., *the Spanish-American War*).

ward   Capitalize only if part of a proper noun (e.g., *Ward Three*).

warhead

warmonger

wartime

war zone

wash-   Compound words beginning with *wash-* are not usually hyphenated (e.g., *washroom*).

washed-out

washed-up

Washington

Washington's Birthday

WASP or Wasp   Acronym for *white Anglo-Saxon Protestant.*

water-   Compound words beginning with *water-* are not usually hyphenated (e.g., *Waterlogged*) and are frequently spelled out as two words (e.g., *water tower*). When in doubt, consult a dictionary.

watershed

waterworks

WATS   Acronym for *wide-area telecommunications service.*

watt-hour

wave band

wavelength

-way   Compound words ending in *-way* are not usually hyphenated (e.g., *causeway*).

ways and means

wea. or wthr.   Abbreviations for *weather.*

weak-minded

week   Capitalize only if part of a proper noun (e.g., *Holy Week*).

well- Compound words beginning with *well-* are usually hyphenated (e.g., *well-wisher*).

wellspring

Welsh rabbit or **Welsh rarebit**

West Virginia   Abbreviation *WV.*

wh.   Abbreviation for *which.*

where- Compound words beginning with *where-* are not usually hyphenated (e.g., *whereabouts*).

white- Compound words beginning with *white-* are not usually hyphenated (e.g., *whitewash*) and are frequently spelled out as two words (e.g., *white flag*). When in doubt, consult a dictionary.

white-hot

whodunit or **whodunnit**   Murder mystery.

whole-hog   As an adverb.

whole hog   As a noun.

whsle. or **whol.**   Abbreviations for *wholesale.*

-wide Compound words ending in *-wide* are not usually hyphenated (e.g., *districtwide*).

wind- Compound words beginning with *wind-* are not usually hyphenated (e.g., *windsail*).

windchill factor

Wisconsin   Abbreviation *WI.*

-wise   Compound words ending in *-wise* are not usually hyphenated (e.g., *edgewise*).

witness-box

witness stand

wk.   Abbreviation for *week.*

wkg.   Abbreviation for *working.*

wkly.   Abbreviation for *weekly.*

wkr.   Abbreviation for *worker.*

w/o   Abbreviation for *without.*

woebegone

wok

wolf; pl. wolves

woman's rights or **women's rights**

women's liberation or **women's lib**

wonderland

wonder-worker

word for word

word-of-mouth   As an adjective.

word of mouth   As a noun.

wordplay

word processor   Abbreviation *WP.*

work-   Compound words beginning with *work-* are not usually hyphenated (e.g., *workshop*).

-work   Compound words ending in *-work* are not usually hyphenated (e.g., *handiwork*).

worker's compensation

work ethic

work force

world-class

World Series

World War

world-weary

wpm   Abbreviation for *words per minute.*

wreak havoc

writer's block

wt.   Abbreviation for *weight.*

Wyoming   Abbreviation *WY.*

X

X-C   Abbreviation for *cross-country*.

X chromosome

x-coordinate

xenophobia

Xerox   Trademarked name for photocopying equipment.

xl or **XL**   Abbrevations for *extra-large*.

Xmas   Abbreviation for *Christmas*.

X-rated   In reference to the movie rating system.

x-ray or **X-ray**   As an adjective or a verb.

x ray or **X ray**   As a noun.

xs or **XS**   Abbreviations for *extra-small*.

xylophone

Y

yak

yams   Not related to sweet potatoes, although these two words are popularly substituted for each other in common parlance in certain regions of the United States.

Yankee

Yankee-Doodle or **Yankee Doodle**

yard sale

Y chromosome

yd. or **y.**   Abbreviations for *yard.*

yeah or **yea**   Variations of the affirmative *yes.*

year   Capitalize only if part of a proper noun (e.g., *New Year's Day*).

yearbook

year-end

year-round

yellow jacket

yellow pages

yest. or **yday.**   Abbreviation for *yesterday.*

yesterday

yesteryear

YMCA   Acronym for *Young Men's Christian Association.*

yogurt or **yoghurt**

Yom Kippur

yoo-hoo

youth; pl. **youths**

yo-yo

yr.   Abbreviation for *year.*

Yukon Territory   Canadian province; abbreviation *YT.*

Yule log

yuppie   Acronym for *young urban professional* or *young, upwardly mobile professional.*

YWCA   Acronym for *Young Women's Christian Association.*

zaftig   Yiddish word meaning "plump."

zenith   The greatest height. Synonyms: *acme; pinnacle.*

zeros or **zeroes**

zigzag

zilch

zinfandel

Zionism

ZIP code   Acronym for *Zone Improvement Program,* which created a five-digit coding system to indicate locale (e.g. *Princeton, NJ 08540*).

zirconia

ziti   This is both the plural and singular term for this type of pasta.

zodiac signs

zodiacal   Of, relating to, or within the zodiac.

zombie

zookeeper

zoot suit   A flashy suit of extreme cut, typically consisting of a thigh-length jacket with wide padded shoulders and peg-top trousers tapering to narrow cuffs. The term was coined in approximately 1910 by Harold C. Fox, an American bandleader and clothier. Forms of the word include *zoot-suiter.*

Zoroastrianism

zucchini

zuppa inglese   An Italian dessert.

zwieback   A type of German bread that is usually sweetened, enriched with eggs, baked, sliced and then toasted until very crisp and dry.

zygo-   Compound words beginning with *zygo-* are not usually hyphenated (e.g., *zygophore; zygomycete; zygocactus; zygogenesis*).

-zygous   Compound words ending in *-zygous* are not usually hyphenated (e.g., *heterozygous; cryptozygous*).

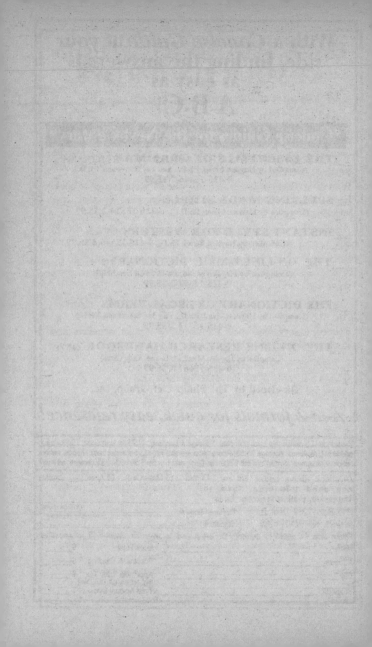